Phil & Caroline

In appreciation

Winnie Mueller

December, 1993

STILL HIGHER
FOR HIS
HIGHEST

STILL HIGHER
FOR HIS
HIGHEST

Devotional Selections for Every Day by
OSWALD CHAMBERS
Author of *My Utmost for His Highest*

WELCH PUBLISHING COMPANY INC.
Burlington, Ontario, Canada

This edition issued by special arrangement with Zondervan Publishing House, Grand Rapids, Michigan.
Original title: STILL HIGHER FOR HIS HIGHEST
Copyright © 1970 by D.W. Lambert

ISBN: 0-920413-19-6

Welch Publishing Company Inc.
960 Gateway
Burlington, Ontario
L7L 5K7   Canada

Printed in Canada

PROLOGUE

Some forty years ago, *My Utmost for His Highest*, Daily Readings from Oswald Chambers, was published and soon became a devotional classic, known and loved by many.

Now the request has come for a further selection from the works of that remarkable spiritual teacher.

Turning over the mass of material available one is inclined to say what Dryden said of Chaucer, 'Here is God's Plenty'. Many of the extracts are from the B.T.C. Journal issued April 1932 and April 1952, also from O. C.'s books already in print. I am especially indebted to Miss Kathleen Chambers for the loan of some hitherto unprinted lecture notes on the Prophets.

Oswald Chambers used to speak of our Lord 'presenting the Truth in nugget form'; while later the apostles 'beat out the nuggets into negotiable gold'. The daily readings given here may be regarded as nuggets of spiritual truth, to be turned into coinage for daily living. The process involves not only prayerful meditation, but, as our author would insist, strenuous thought and spiritual concentration.

May the Holy Spirit quicken and enlighten all who use this book.

D. W. L.

An index of Scripture references is provided at the
end of this volume.

Can You See the Highest?

Psalm 18: 16; Ephesians 2: 6

The Lord Jesus Christ is the Highest. Is there anyone else higher to you than He is? Your life is never safeguarded until Jesus is seen to be the Highest. Past experience will not keep you, neither will deliverance from sin; the only safeguarding power is The Highest. If there is a breath of confidence anywhere else, there will be disaster, and it is by the mercy of God that you are allowed to stumble, or to be pain-smitten, until you learn that He does it all—*He* keeps you from stumbling, *He* raises you up and keeps you up, *He* sends from above and delivers you. "Now unto Him that is able to keep you from falling. . . ."

Whenever there is a complication in your circumstances, do nothing until you see the Highest—not sometimes, but always (cf. Isaiah 50: 10). Can you see the Lord in your thinking? If not, suspend your judgment until you can. Can you see the face of Jesus in your affections? If not, restrain them until you can. Can you see God in your circumstances? If not, do nothing until you can. Our Lord can trust anything to the man or woman who sees Him.

Are You Succoured by the Highest?

Isaiah 61: 1, 2; Philippians 2: 1, 2

Until a worker knows the succour of God, he is in danger of becoming a stumbling block to other souls. If we are not being succoured by the Highest, of what use can we be to those folks who are crushed by sorrows of which we know nothing? "The sacrifices of God are a broken heart" broken beyond any patching up, but— "He hath sent Me to bind up the broken-hearted." The heart which has been bound up and succoured by the Lord Jesus Christ will never be got on the train of self-interest, there is no selfishness left in it. "As one whom his mother comforteth, so will I comfort you." That is the most powerful thing God can do for us. The great note of the life which is comforted of God is—"For my Lord I live; by my Lord I am strengthened, and in my Lord I am succoured."

The Greatest Good Is the Highest End

Matthew 7: 11–14

The Shorter Catechism states, in answer to the question, "What is man's chief end?" that "Man's chief end is to glorify God and enjoy Him for ever." It is not what man puts into his body or on his body, but what he brings out of his body (cf. Matthew 15: 17–20), and what he brings out of what he puts on his body, viz. his money, that reveals what he considers his chief end. A great many people imagine they have glorified God when they have given two halfpennies for a penny, or have saved a halfpenny. The highest good to them is to keep economic relations right, the highest Good from Jesus Christ's standpoint never dawns on them. The craze to-day is that the highest good is what a man has to live on: feed him, keep his body healthy, and his moral and religious life will be all right. That is the highest good according to the standard of many. As Christians it is more important to know how to live than what to live on.

The Greatest Good Is the Highest Evangel

Matthew 7: 21

To apply the rule of the kingdom of God to our daily life is done not by our heads but by the obedience of our hearts. "If you are ever going to get the true blessedness," says Jesus, "it must be by living your life according to the rule of God." How are we going to discern the rule of God? Jesus told Nicodemus: "If you are born from above you will *see* the kingdom of God, and *enter into it*" (John 3: 3, 5). Then after we have entered into the kingdom of God, are we going to apply its rule to our bodily life, our mental life, our spiritual life? We are at liberty to stop short at any point, and our Lord will never cast it up at us; but think what we shall feel like when we see Him if all the 'thank you' we gave Him for His unspeakable salvation was an obstinate determination to serve Him in our own way, not His.

Heart in the Heavens, Feet on Earth
Ephesians 2: 3-6

Being seated together in heavenly places in Christ Jesus does not mean lolling about on the mount of transfiguration, singing ecstatic hymns, and letting demon-possessed boys go to the devil in the valley; it means being in the accursed places of this earth as far as the walk of the feet is concerned but in undisturbed communion with God.

". . . while we look not at the things which are seen"—that battle never stops. The things that are seen are not the devil but the pressing things, the things that distract; when Christ is formed in us and the essential vision comes through looking at the things which are not seen, we find that God makes other people shadows. If my saintly friends are images of God to me, I have much further to go yet. God alone must be my Stay and Source and everything. That is the way the godly life is lived.

Is God Really First?
Matthew 6: 33

The great curse of modern Christianity is that people will not be careless about things they have no right to be careful about, and they will not let God make them careful about their relationship to Him. Sum it up for yourself—what do you think about most, not on the surface, but in the deep centre of your being? What is the real basal thought of your life—"what ye shall eat, what ye shall drink, what ye shall put on"? None of us are so stupid or lacking in cunning as to say we do not think of these things: but if we think of what will happen to 'all these things' if we put God first, we know where we are. If He is first you know you can never think of anything He will forget.

Are We Letting God Work?

John 5: 17

What we have to do, and what God cannot do, is to work out what He has worked in. We try to do God's work for Him, and God has to wait until we are passive enough to let Him work in us. To believe in Jesus means retiring and letting God take the mastership inside. That is all God asks of us. Have we ever got into the way of letting God work, or are we so amazingly important that we really wonder what the Almighty does before we are up in the morning! We are so certain we know what is right, and if we don't always keep at it God cannot get on. Compare that view with the grand, marvellous working of God in the life of the Lord Jesus. Our Lord did not work for God; He said, "The Father that dwelleth in Me, He doeth the works."

Redemption, God's Final Purpose

Colossians 1: 19, 20

The truth about God is Jesus Christ—light, life and love. Whatever is dark to us will, by means of our obedience, become as clear as the truth which we have made ours by obedience. The bit we do know is the most glorious, unfathomable delight conceivable, and that is going to be true about everything to do with God and us. The process is continual obedience.

The world is for redemption, not for progress, and a Christian is one who has been taken into that secret by the personal experience of Redemption. It is a continual revelation centring round one thing, the Cross of God in Jesus Christ, and the characteristic is that we have to be crucified too, and live only the life 'hid with Christ in God.'

Obeying the Heavenly Vision

Acts 26: 19

"But rise, and stand upon thy feet: for I have appeared unto thee for this purpose, to make thee a minister and a witness both of these things which thou hast seen, and of those things in which I will appear unto thee" (Acts 26: 16).

We all have visions, if we are spiritual at all, of what Jesus Christ wants. When we are born again and come into contact with Him, we know what He wants us to be, and the great thing is to learn how not to be disobedient to the vision, not say it cannot be attained. Verse 16 is immensely commanding; there is nothing there apart from the personal relationship. Paul was not given a message or a doctrine, nor a direction of thought; he was brought into a vivid, personal, overmastering relationship to Jesus Christ.

Defiling the Temple

1 Corinthians 3: 17

That truth applied to us individually means this—once realize that your body is the temple of the Holy Ghost, and you can never again do with success what you once did, the slightest attempt to do so brings a painful realization of Paul's words in 1 Corinthians 3: 17—"If any man destroyeth the temple of God, him shall God destroy." I have no jurisdiction over my body, there is only one honour at stake, the honour of God. Defiling the temple of the Holy Ghost is the result of my exercising my right to myself; realizing this made Paul say, "I buffet my body and bring it into bondage: lest by any means, after that I have preached to others, I myself should be rejected."

The True Work of the True Church

Ephesians 5: 27; Revelation 2: 5

Jesus Christ has done a work we cannot do, and the manifestation of that glorious finished work is seen in every man and woman who stands on that finished work in conscious committing faith. The Church ('that which is called out') is called out to proclaim what Jesus Christ has done and can do, to stand backed by Almighty God for strong, stern, surgical, spiritual salvation and sanctification. The Church is not called to success, the Church is called to deliver God's message and to be for the praise of His glory. Her one desire is to be the fitted Bride of Christ, "without spot, or wrinkle, or any such thing." The Church must stand for the GLORY OF GOD and for what God can do—not as a socialistic institution under the patronage of God. The voice of the Lord cries again to-day—"Remember therefore from whence thou art fallen, and repent, and do the first works; or else I will come in to thee quickly and will remove thy candlestick out of its place, except thou repent."

Are We Willing to Come to Him?

Matthew 11: 28

Our Lord's marvellous message for all time is familiar: "Come unto Me . . . and I will give you rest." "The wayfaring men, yea fools, shall not err therein." When a man does err in the way of God, it is because he is wise in his own conceits. When the facts of life have humbled us, when introspection has stripped us of our own miserable self-interest and we receive a startling diagnosis of ourselves by the Holy Spirit, we are by that painful experience brought to the place where we can hear the marvellous message—profounder than the profoundest philosophies earth ever wove, "Come until Me, all ye that labour and are heavy laden, and I will give you rest." Until this experience comes men may patronize Jesus Christ, but they do not come to Him for salvation. The only solution is the one given by Jesus Christ Himself to a good upright man of His day: "Marvel not that I say unto thee, ye must be born from above."

January 13th

The Standard, 'As I Have Loved You'

John 13: 34

Remember the standard, *'as I have loved you.'* I wonder where the best of us are according to that standard? How many of us have turned away over and over again in disgust at men, and when we get alone with the Lord Jesus He speaks no word, but the memory of Him is quite sufficient to bring the rebuke—"as I have loved you." It takes severe training to think habitually along the lines Jesus Christ has laid down, although we act on them impulsively at times.

January 14th

The Tragedy of the Backslider

Jeremiah 12: 9

"Is mine heritage unto me as a speckled bird of prey?" This is not a picture of a saint living a holy life in the world; it is the picture of a saint who is leaving God and going into the world, with the result that the birds of prey, i.e. those who have never recognized God, are tearing that life to bits, and God does not protect it. That is the thing that staggered Jeremiah. God is bringing him to see the reason: the people have rebelled against Him. If I backslide, I take some of the glorious plumage of the heritage of God with me, and as it gets bedraggled I am torn to pieces by the people who never knew Jesus Christ.

"Many shepherds have destroyed my vineyard, . . . no man layeth it to heart." God would have been 'a wall of fire round about and the glory in the midst' if they had been obedient. The difference between God as a consuming fire and natural fire is just this, that the further you get away from God the more fiercely you feel His burnings, but when you are close to Him, you find it is a glorious protection.

January 15th
The Supernatural Lord Comes in Common Ways
John 1: 38, 39, 40

There is something so natural and yet so supernatural about Jesus. We never read that Jesus button-holed anybody; these men came to Him and asked, "Master, where do you live?" He said "Come, and ye shall see"—obvious and simple, yet full of Divine power. The difference between the Christianity stamped by the Holy Ghost and that stamped by ecstacy and fanaticism is just here, the one makes the supernatural 'spooky' and puts the natural nowhere; the other makes the supernatural natural. Jesus does not come to men in extraordinary ways, but in the most ordinary things—washing disciples' feet; preparing breakfast; at a wedding feast. The early disciples were not attracted to Jesus because of their sense of sin, they were religious men, in touch with the elemental forces of nature, simple and unconventional, and when they saw Jesus their spirit indicated at once "This is the very One we have been looking for."

January 16th
The Wonder of Faith
Hebrews 11: 27 (R.V.)

Faith cannot be intellectually defined; faith is the inborn capacity to see God behind everything, the wonder that keeps you an eternal child. What is your faith to you—a wonderful thing, or a bandbox thing? Satisfaction is too often the peace of death; wonder is the very essence of life. Beware always of losing the wonder, and the first thing that stops wonder is religious conviction. Whenever you give a trite testimony the wonder is gone. The only evidence of salvation or sanctification is that the sense of wonder is developing, not at things as they are, but at the One who made them as they are. There is no set definition of faith into which you can fit these men and women; they were heroes of faith because they "endured, as seeing Him who is invisible."

The Discipline of Love

1 Corinthians 13

1 Corinthians 13 is the description of how Christianity works out in a man's actual experience. Love is the sovereign preference of my person for another; my love for Jesus Christ means that I deliberately identify myself with His interests in other people—and the Lord is interested in some funny folk. Jesus Christ demands, if I am born from above and have inherited His disposition, that I show it, not to fictitious people, but to the people I live beside. Our Heavenly Father has an amazing sense of humour; He will bring across your path the kind of people who manifest to you what you have been to Him. If you have been obstinate, that is why you have got that fellow around you just now, and Jesus says, "Show him the attitude I showed you." That is experimental Christianity with no humbug. It means showing the disposition of Jesus Christ to the man who deliberately wrongs you, and it takes some doing.

Spiritual Instability

James 1: 8

Our Lord refers to this instability in His parable of the sower and the seed—"they receive the word gladly, but they have no root in themselves"—quicksilver Christians. They may have as many conversions as there are days in the year, and at the end of the year remain the same unreliable emotional people, utterly incapable of resting in a stable point of truth, and they become eager adherents of every new interest. The main characteristic of young modern life to-day is an intense craving to be interested. Literature, amusements, all indicate this tendency, and in religion the Church is apt to pander to the demand to be interested; consequently men won't face the rugged facts of the Gospel because when the Holy Spirit comes in He challenges a man's will, demands a reconstruction of his whole life, and produces a change of mind which will work havoc in his former complacency.

The True Prophet Identified With Sin

Ezekiel 3: 16, 17

"And it came to pass at the end of seven days, that the word of the Lord came unto me, saying, Son of man, I have made thee a watchman unto the house of Israel: . . ." Ezekiel, in common with all the Old Testament prophets, had not to generate his message out of his own individuality, he had simply to obey God. The obedient life is stated for us in Matthew 11: 25 and 1 John 1: 7, simplicity and single unfoldedness before God. Do I believe in God, or in a wise and understanding way of doing God's work? The message God laid on Ezekiel to deliver found no natural affinity for itself in him; the message was built on a supernatural affinity with God. God mortifies our affinities that limit Him. Like the apostle Paul, Ezekiel has a "Woe is unto me, if I preach not the gospel;" he had a commission to warn the people of God, not win them, and he was to speak according to God's discretion, not according to his own judgment.

The Failure of Mere Temperament

Job 2: 13

Temperamental—the way a man looks at life. My temperament is an inner disposition which influences my thoughts and actions to a certain extent, i.e., I am either pessimistic or optimistic according to the way my blood circulates. It is an insult to take the temperamental line in dealing with human beings—"Cheer up, look on the bright side;" there are some types of suffering before which the only thing you can do is to keep your mouth shut. There are times when a man needs to be handled by God, not by his fellow men, and part of the gift of man's wisdom is to know how to be reverent with what he does not understand.

The Disasters of Fellowship With Him

2 Corinthians 1: 8, 9

There are disasters to be faced by the one who is in real fellowship with the Lord Jesus Christ. God has never promised to keep us immune from trouble; He says "I will be with him in trouble," which is a very different thing. Paul was "an apostle of Jesus Christ by the will of God," and it is this fact that accounts for the crushing criticism and the spiteful treatment to which he was subjected by those who could not discern on what authority he based his apostleship. That was the ground Paul stood on, and that only—he was an apostle *"by the will of God" (see* Col. 1: 1).

If you are experiencing the disasters of fellowship, don't get into despair, remain unswervingly and unhesitatingly faithful to the Lord Jesus Christ and refuse to compromise for one second.

Thinking About Men as Jesus Thought

Matthew 24: 12

It is easy if you are an innocent person to be shocked at immorality, but how much education in the school of Christ, how much reliance on the Holy Spirit, does it take to bring us to the place where we are shocked at pride against God?

The Spirit of God can bring us into sympathy with the work Jesus has done. "And because iniquity shall abound, the love of many shall wax cold." Jesus Christ sketched the portrait of many of us in those words twenty centuries ago. Think of the worst man or woman you ever knew—not the worst man or woman you can think of because that is vague—have you any hope for him? for her? That is the test as to whether or not you have been learning to think about men as Jesus thought of them. Does the Holy Spirit begin to convey to your mind the wonder of "that man, that woman, being 'presented perfect in Christ Jesus' "?

Is Life and Conduct Right?

Matthew 5: 24

Many a powerless, fruitless Christian life has resulted from some insignificant thing—'*first go.*' The thing that fights longest against the Spirit of God's demands is my prideful claim to my right to myself, which is the essence of sin. It is extraordinary what we are brought up against when the Spirit of God is at work in us; the only sign of regeneration in practical experience is that we begin to make our life in accordance with the principles of God. Am I prepared to be identified with the death of Jesus morally? The Holy Spirit will drive it home—am I going to see that my goods are up to sample, that my back premises are in keeping with the shop window? am I trying to put a snowdrift over a rubbish heap, or am I going to wash myself white in the blood of the Lamb? If I have received the Holy Spirit, I must show it, the thing must be visible all through. If Jesus Christ cannot alter a man's disposition, Christianity is a cunningly devised fable. Christianity means the manifestation of a strong family likeness to Jesus.

Why Did Jesus Offend?

Matthew 13: 57

"He is despised and rejected of men." Jesus offended many; His own home folk were the first to be offended. "And when His friends heard of it, they went out to lay hold on Him: for they said, He is beside Himself"—"He assumes too much for His humble position." When he preached in the synagogue, they were astonished, but— "Is not this the carpenter? . . . And they were offended at Him." The Jews were offended at Jesus because they looked for a warrior king in their coming Messiah, and the carelessness of Jesus over temporal positions and honour did not commend itself to them. The Pharisees were offended at Him because His teaching showed up the hollow emptiness of their profession. His own disciples were offended at Him—"All ye shall be offended in Me this night."

January 25th

Claiming All Sufficient Grace

2 Corinthians 9: 8

When God brings us up against difficult circumstances that reveal the inability of our human nature it is not that we may sink back and say, "Oh dear, I thought I should have been all right by now;" it is that we may learn to drawn on our union with Jesus Christ and claim that we have sufficient grace to do this particular thing according to God's will. If we are vitally connected with God in our thinking we shall find we can walk; but if we have not been thinking rightly we will succumb—"I cannot do this." If we are thinking along the line of God's grace, that He is able to make all grace abound unto us, we will not only stand, but walk as a son or daughter of God and prove that His grace is sufficient. To be weak in God's strength is a crime.

January 26th

The Offence of the Cross and the Blood

1 Corinthians 1: 23

'Blood' was, and is, the offence. "You Christians wallow in blood," it is objected, "could no other word be used? There is something so offensive in the word 'blood.' And why talk so much about sin? Sin is but a defect, slowly being outgrown in the evolution of man." 'Blood,' the vital life-stream—offensive! is there nothing offensive in sin, that devastating thing which poisons the very fountain of life, which makes the world a howling wilderness and our cities unendurable to thought—a defect! The evolutionary idea sounds all right; it is the thinker himself who is wrong. Sin has alienated man from God and the story of the ages is an accumulation of wrongdoing and of judgment days; there is utter hopelessness in any attempt to meet the righteousness of God; but let a man begin to realize what sin is, then *"the blood of Jesus Christ His Son cleanseth us from all sin"* will be a holy word to his soul. 'The Cross' and 'the blood of Jesus' are indeed names for profound mysteries, but when a soul shattered by the crushing sense of his guilt believes that through the blood of Jesus there is forgiveness for sin, he receives a new life-energy, he is purged from his old sins.

The Recognition of Deity

Matthew 16: 16

Immediately you lose sight of the central, majestic Figure of Jesus Christ, you are swept off your feet by all kinds of doctrine; and when big things hit us we find that our religion does not stand us in good stead; our creed does not agree with Jesus Christ.

The revelation of the Deity of Christ does not come to a man's intellect first, but to his heart and life, and he says with amazement, "Thou art the Christ, the Son of the living God." The great point of the Bible revelation of God is not only that God was in Christ but that Jesus Christ is God. "He that hath seen Me hath seen the Father," said Jesus. If Jesus Christ is not God, then the only God we have is an abstraction of our own minds.

Stablished by Faith That Receives

Colossians 2: 6, 7

"And stablished by your faith." Think of the things you are trying to have faith for! Stop thinking of them and think about your state in God through receiving Christ Jesus; see how God has enabled you to walk where you used to totter, and see what marvellous strength you have in Him. "I can do all things in Him that strengthened me," says Paul. Is that mere poetry or a fact? Paul never talked poetry only. All the great blessings of God in salvation and sanctification, all the Holy Spirit's illumination, are ours not because we obey, they are ours because we have put ourselves into a right relationship with God by receiving Christ Jesus, and we obey spontaneously. As we look back we find that every time we have been blessed it was not through mechanical obedience, but by receiving from Jesus something that enabled us to obey without knowing it, and life was flooded with the power of God. We make it hard for people—Do this and that, and they obey and nothing happens. We have left out altogether the receiving of Christ Jesus the Lord; we have to be rooted and built up in Him.

'Eating' at God's Command

Ezekiel 3: 1–3

The conception of 'swallowing' a word of God has in it the essence of obedience. There is no room for debate when God speaks. Obedience is never the outcome of intellectual discernment, it springs from moral simplicity, keeping in the light of God. "Eat this roll" —an unpalatable thing to do, but Ezekiel obeyed, "and it was in my mouth as honey for sweetness." Obedience to a word of God always brings an amazing sweetness to the life of the obeyer. Over and over again God brings us up to a word of His, e.g., the conditions of discipleship (Luke 14: 26), and we say, "Oh, I couldn't possibly 'swallow' that," and we nibble at it and run away from it, and God brings us back to it again and again until we are willing to obey; immediately we obey and appropriate the word it becomes 'as honey for sweetness.'

January 30th

Our Civilization and Christ's Call

Matthew 6: 33

To follow Jesus Christ to-day is to follow a madman according to the ideals of present-day civilization. We have made a thousand and one necessities until our system of civilized life is as cast-iron, and then we apologize to the Lord for not following Him. "God can never mean that I have to follow Him at the cost of all I have?" But He does mean it. Instantly the clash is between our civilization and the call of Jesus Christ. Read the Sermon on the Mount—"Seek ye first the kingdom of God"—and apply it to modern life and you will find its statements are either those of a madman or of God Incarnate.

Unbelief Hinders God's Work

Matthew 13: 58

The basis of human life is not rational, but redemptive, consequently it ought to be an easy thing for the Christian who thinks to conceive of any and every type of man being presented perfect in Christ Jesus. But how seldom we do think! If I am an earnest evangelical preacher I may say to a man, "Oh yes, God can save you," while in my own heart I don't believe there is much hope for him. Our unbelief stands as the supreme barrier to Christ's work in men's souls. "And He did not many mighty works there because of their unbelief." Once let me get over my own slowness of heart to believe in Jesus Christ's power to save and I become a real generator of His power to men. "Neither is there salvation in any other; for there is none other name under heaven given among men, whereby we must be saved."

Regeneration

2 Peter 1: 4

All through the Bible the authority of God's law is unflinchingly revealed; but along with man's responsibility to meet that demand comes the revelation of Regeneration, viz., that we can be regenerated into a life in which the holiness of Almighty God is imparted to us. It is God's own holiness that is given to us, not the power to imitate His holiness, but the very nature of God is imparted to us. We are "presenced with divinity"; "made partakers of the divine nature." God becomes incarnated in us through the Redemption. The Bible reveals that Jesus Christ, Who was God Incarnate, has lifted the whole human race on to another plane of responsibility; and on that plane our responsibility does not lie in being absolutely holy, but in seeing that we allow God to be absolutely holy in us.

Wearing Saul's Armour

1 Samuel 17: 38, 39

"If your religion injures your intelligence, it is bad; if it injures your character, it is vicious; if it injures your conscience, it is criminal." (Amiel.)

Therefore don't try and wear Saul's armour. It is pathetic to see us when we are about a month old in grace trying to wear the terrific armour of mature saints; we go about clanking great sentiments on profound themes while our practical life laughs at us. If we obey God, He will introduce us by the current of events and by our obedience into the place where these truths become real to us, and we begin to 'grow up into Him in all things.' Anything that relieves us from personal accountability to Jesus Christ is corrupt.

Discipline of the Body

1 Corinthians 9: 27

The forming of new habits is difficult until you get into the way of doing it, then everything you meet with aids you in developing along the right line. It is good practice to sit down for five minutes and do nothing; in that way you will soon discover how little control you have over yourself. In forming a new habit it is vitally important to insist on bringing the body under control first. Paul says, "I maul and master my body, in case, after preaching to others, I am disqualified myself." The natural man is created by God as well as the new man in Christ, and the new man has to be manifested by the natural man in his mortal flesh.

Discipline of the Mind

Philippians 4: 5

Our thinking processes are largely subject to the law of habit. "Let your forbearance," i.e., self-control, "be made known unto all men." Self-control is nothing more than a mental habit which controls the body and mind by a dominant relationship, viz.: the immediate presence of the Lord—"for the Lord is at hand." The danger in spiritual matters is that we do not *think* godliness; we let ideas and conceptions of godliness lift us up at times, but we do not form the habit of godly thinking. Thinking godliness cannot be done in spurts, it is a steady habitual trend. God does not give us our physical or mental habits; He gives us the power to form any kind of habits we like, and in the spiritual domain we have to form the habit of godly thinking.

Meditate on These Things

1 Tim. 4: 15

"Meditate upon these things." Meditation means getting to the middle of a thing, pinning yourself down to a certain thing and concentratedly brooding upon it. The majority of us attend only to the 'muddle' of things, consequently we get spiritual indigestion, the counterpart of physical indigestion, a desperately gloomy state of affairs. We cannot see anything rightly, and all we do see is stars. "Faith is the evidence of things not seen." Suppose Jesus suddenly lifted the veil from our eyes and let us see angels ministering to us, His own presence with us, the Holy Ghost in us, and the Father around us; how amazed we should be! We have lived in the 'muddle' instead of in the middle of things. Faith gets us into the middle, which is God and God's purpose. "Lord, I pray Thee, open his eyes, that he may see;" and when his eyes were opened he saw the hosts of God and nothing else (2 Kings 6: 16).

Deliverance From Misunderstanding

Psalm 73: 23–25

The first thing a Christian is emancipated from is the tyranny of moods and the tyranny of feeling he is not understood. These things are the most fruitful sources of misery. Half the misery in the world comes because one person demands of another a complete understanding, which is absolutely impossible. The only Being Who understands us is the Being Who made us. It is a tremendous emancipation to get rid of every kind of self-consideration and learn to heed only one thing, the relationship between God and ourselves. "In all the world there is none but thee, my God, there is none but thee." Once we get there, other people become shadows, beautiful shadows, but shadows under God's control.

Prayer, an Effort of the Will

John 15: 7

"Enter into thy closet, and when thou hast shut thy door, pray to thy Father which is in secret." Prayer that is not an effort of the will is unrecognized by God. "Ye shall ask what ye *will*," said Jesus. That does not mean ask anything you like, but what you *will*. What are you actively willing? Ask for that. We shall find that we *ask* very few things. The tendency in prayer to leave ourselves all abroad to the influence of a meeting or a special season is not scriptural. Prayer is an effort of will, and Jesus Christ instructs us by using the word 'ask.' "Everyone that asketh receiveth." These words are an amazing revelation of the simplicity with which God would have us pray.

February 8th

Neglect Not the Gift

1 Timothy 4: 14

"Neglect not the gift that is in thee." We have to be careful not to neglect the spiritual reality planted in us by God. The first thing that contact with reality does is to enable us to diagnose our moods. It is a great moment when we realize that we have the power to trample on certain moods. Moods never go by praying, moods go by kicking. A mood nearly always has its seat in the physical condition, not in the moral, and it is a continual effort to refuse to listen to those moods which arise from a physical condition; we must not submit to them for a second. It is a great thing to have something to neglect in your life; a great thing for your moral character to have something to snub. "The expulsive power of a new affection"—that is what Christianity supplies. The Spirit of God on the basis of Redemption gives us something else to think about. Are we going to think about it?

February 9th

Where Do You Live?

Psalm 91: 1

No one can tell you where the shadow of the Almighty is, you must find that out for yourself. When you have found out where it is, stay there; under that shadow no evil can ever befall you. The intensity of the moments spent under the shadow of the Almighty is the measure of your usefulness as a worker. Intensity of communion is not in feelings or emotions or in special places, but in quiet, fixed, confident centring on God. Never allow anything to hinder you from being in the place where your spiritual life is maintained.

Sent of God

Romans 10: 15

The Christian worker must be sent; he must not elect to go. Nowadays that is the last thing thought of; it is a determination on the part of the individual.—This is something I can do and I am going to do it. Beware of demanding that people go into work, it is a craze; the majority of saved souls are not fit to feed themselves yet. How am I to know I have been sent of God? First, by the realization that I am utterly weak and powerless and if I am to be of any use to God, God must do it all the time.—Is this the humiliating certainty of my soul, or merely a sentimental phrase? Second, because I know I have to point men to Jesus Christ, not get them to think what a holy man I am. The only way to be sent is to let God lift us right out of any sense of fitness in ourselves and place us where He will.

Discerning Through Doing

John 7: 17

Jesus says we shall know, i.e., discern, whether His teaching is of God or not when we do what we know to be His Will. We discern according to our disposition. There are moments in life when the little thing matters more than anything else, times when a critical situation depends upon our attitude of mind to another person. If a man is hesitating between obeying and not obeying God, the tiniest thing contrary to obedience is quite sufficient to swing the pendulum right away from the discernment of Jesus Christ and of God. "If thou bring thy gift to the altar, and there rememberest that thy brother hath ought against thee . . . *first go*." Distempers of mind make all the difference in the discernment of Jesus Christ's teaching. Have I a distempered view about any man or woman on earth? If I have, there is a great deal of Jesus Christ's teaching I do not want to listen to; then I will never discern His teaching.

God's Final Word
Matthew 16: 17, 18

Our Lord's teaching is God-breathed. What makes the difference between the attitude of a spiritual Christian to the teaching of Jesus and that of an unspiritual person? An unspiritual person takes the statements of Jesus to pieces as he would any man's, he dissolves Him by analysis (1 John 4: 3). A spiritual Christian never does. The basis of membership of the early Church was discernment of Who Jesus is by the revelation of God (Matthew 16: 17-18). All through that is the test—Do I know Who Jesus Christ is, and do I know that His teaching is of God?

The mystery of the Bible is that its inspiration was direct from God. (2 Peter 1: 21). To believe Our Lord's consciousness about Himself commits me to accept Him as God's last endless Word. That does not mean that God is not still speaking, but it does mean that He is saying nothing different from the Final Word, Jesus Christ. All God says expounds that Word.

Supremacy Over Our Enemies
Psalm 18: 37-40

The supremacy over our old enemies is accounted for by the fact that God makes them our subjects. What were your enemies? Stodginess of head, laziness of body or spirit, the whole vocabulary of "I can'ts." When you live in the right place these things are made your subjects. The things that used to hinder your life with God become subject to you by His power. The very things that used to upset you now minister to you in an extraordinary way by reason of the spiritual supremacy God gives you over them. The life of a saint reveals a quietness at the heart of things, there is something firm and dependable, because the Lord is the strength of the life.

God in the Unconscious

Romans 8: 26, 27

The first moment of thinking alters our life. If for one moment we have discerned the truth, we can never be the same again. We may ignore it, or forget it, but it will not forget us. Truth once discerned goes down into the subconscious mind, but it will jump up in a most awkward way when we don't want it to. In the matter of intercession, when we pray for another the Spirit of God works in the unconscious domain of that one's being about which we know nothing, and about which the one we pray for knows nothing; and after a while the conscious life of the one prayed for begins to show signs of softening and unrest, of enquiry and a desire to know something. It seems stupid to think that if we pray for all that will happen, but remember to Whom we pray. We pray to a God Who understands the unconscious depths of a man's personality, and He has told us to pray.

The World and the Church

Ephesians 5: 27; 1 John 5: 19

The Church confronts the world with a message the world craves for but resents because it comes through the Cross of Christ. The central keystone for all Time and Eternity on which the whole purpose of God depends is the Cross (Gal. 6: 14). When the world gets in a bad way, she refers to the Church; when prosperous, she hates it. If men could blot out the standard of the Christian Church they would do it; but in a crisis they find a need in their own heart. As preachers we are privileged by God to stand stedfast against any element that lowers His standard. We are called upon to confront the world with the Gospel of Christ, not to start off on side tracks of our own. The Church owns a mastery the world can neither ignore nor do without, the mastery of the Lord Jesus Christ.

The Witness of the Preacher

John 3: 30

A preacher must remember that his calling is different from every other calling in life; his personality has to be submerged in his message (cf. John 3: 30). An orator has to work *with* men and enthuse them; a New Testament preacher has to come *upon* men with a message they resent and will not listen to at first. The Gospel comes in with a backing of Divine authority and an arrestment that men resent. There is something in every man that resents the interference of God. Before a man can be saved, the central citadel of his being has to be stormed and taken possession of by the Holy Spirit. It is easy to tell men they must be saved and filled with the Holy Ghost; but we have to live amongst men and show them what a life filled with the Holy Ghost ought to be. A preacher has to come upon men with a message and a testimony that go together. The great pattern for every witness is the abiding Witness, the Lord Jesus Christ.

When He Is Come . . .

John 16: 13, 14

There are some things that are without meaning for us. For instance, to be told that God will give us the Holy Spirit if we ask Him, is a dead proposition; but when we come in contact with a person filled with the Spirit of God we instantly awaken to a want. Or again, if you tell half a dozen clean living upright sterling men that God so loved them that He gave His Son to die for them, only their good breeding will keep them from being amused—Why should Jesus Christ die for me? It is not a living proposition to them, not in the sphere of their life at all. Their morality is well within their own grasp, they are clean living and upright, all that can be desired; they will never be awakened in that way; but present them with Jesus Christ, or with a life that is like His life, and instantly there will awaken in them a want they were not conscious of before.

The Snare of the Sentimentalist

Luke 9: 57, 62

"Lord I will follow Thee, but . . ." The wish ought to be followed by immediate obedience. I must take the wish and translate it into resolution and then into action. If I do not the wish will translate itself into a corrupting instead of a redeeming power in my life. This principle holds good in the matter of emotions. A sentimentalist is one who delights to have high and devout emotions stirred whilst reading in an arm-chair or when in a prayer meeting, but he never translates his emotions into action. Consequently a sentimentalist is usually callous, self-centred and selfish, because the emotions he likes to have stirred do not cost him anything; and when he comes across the same things in the domain where things are real and not sentimental, the revenge comes along the line of selfishness and meanness, which is always the aftermath of an unfulfilled emotion.

Ownership

1 Corinthians 6: 19

The instinct of ownership is seen from the first of life to the last. As soon as an infant tongue can say anything, it will say 'me' and 'mine'. "Is this mine?" "Yes," then expect to see it smashed. The child wishes you to understand that he can do what he likes with his own. It is only the discipline of life that teaches us to keep things. The instinct of ownership is a right one, though the disposition expressed through it may be wrong. In a saint the idea of ownership is that we have the power to 'glorify God by good works.' What we own is the honour of Jesus Christ. Have I ever realized that His honour is at stake in my bodily life? "What? know ye not that your body is the temple of the Holy Ghost which is in you?" Do I own my body for that one purpose? my brain to think God's thoughts after Him? We have to be intensely and personally God's.

Our Victory Through His

John 16: 33

I am only healthy according to the fighting corpuscles in my blood. When the fighting millions inside get low, I become diseased and after a while I shall be snuffed out. Morally it is the same, we are not born moral, we are born innocent and ignorant; morality is the outcome of fight. Immediately I am lazy in moral matters, I become immoral. Spiritually it is the same. "In the world ye shall have tribulation," i.e. everything that is not spiritual makes for our undoing; but, "be of good cheer, I have overcome the world." Why did not Our Lord say that He would help us to overcome? Because we have to imitate Him through the power He has put in us. Think of sitting in a corner before the Almighty and saying, "But my difficulties are so enormous." Thank God they are! The bigger the difficulty, the more amazing is your profit to Jesus Christ as you draw on His supernatural grace.

Prayer and Labour

Matthew 9: 38

"Pray ye therefore the Lord of the harvest, that He send forth labourers into His harvest." Mark the significance of the term 'labour'. We refuse to pray unless we get thrills. May God save us from that counterfeit of true prayer, it is the intensest form of spiritual selfishness. We have to *labour*, and to labour along the line of His direction. Jesus Christ says—*Pray*. It looks stupid; but when we labour at prayer, results happen all the time from His standpoint, because God creates something in answer to, and by means of prayer, that was not in existence before. 'Labour.' It is the one thing we will not do. We will take open-air meetings, we will preach— but labour at prayer! There is nothing thrilling about a labouring man's work, but it is the labouring man who makes the conceptions of the genius possible; and it is the labouring saint who makes the conceptions of his Master possible.

The Prayers of the Saints

Revelation 5: 8

Are we adding to the prayers of the saints or becoming sulky with God if He does not give us what we want, so taken up with the 'nobility of man' that we forget what our calling is as saints? As saints we are called to go through the heroism of what we believe, not of stating what we believe, but of standing by it when the facts are dead against God. It is easy to say 'God is love' when all is going well, but face a woman who has gone through bereavement and see if you find it easy to say it. There is suffering which staggers your mind as you watch it, and yet those who go through it are sustained in a way we do not understand. All day lives are passing by us; how much of the silence of heaven have we broken up by our prayers for them?

Why Give Things Up?

Genesis 22: 2; Romans 12: 1

Abraham is taught by God by the ancient ritual what Paul clearly expressed in Romans 12: 1. Many of us think that God wants us to give up things. God purified Abraham from this blunder, and the same discipline goes on in our lives. "Oh, well, I expect God will ask me to give that up." God nowhere tells us to give up things for the sake of giving them up, He tells us to give them up for the sake of the only thing worth having, viz. life with Himself. It is a question of loosening the bands that hinder our life, and immediately those bands are loosened by identification with the death of Jesus, we enter into a relationship with God whereby we sacrifice our life to God. To give God my life for death is of no value; what is of value is to let Him have all my powers that have been saved and sanctified, so that as Jesus sacrificed His life for His Father, I can sacrifice my life for Him. "Present your bodies a *living* sacrifice," says Paul.

Faith Triumphant

Genesis 22: *11, 12*

The great point of Abraham's faith in God was that he was prepared to do anything for God. Mark the difference between that and doing anything to *prove* your love to God. Abraham was there to obey God, no matter to what he went contrary. Abraham was not a pledged devotee of his own convictions, or he would have slain his son and said the voice of the angel was the voice of the devil. There is always the point of giving up convictions and traditional beliefs. If I will remain true to God, He will lead me straight through the ordeal into the inner chamber of a better knowledge of God. Our Lord taught us to pray "lead us not into temptation." Don't ask God to test you. Don't declare as Peter did, I will do anything, I will go to death for You. Abraham did not make any such declaration, he remained true to God, and God purified his faith.

Hide in His Pavilion

Psalm 27: *1, 5*

God gives us the energy of an impregnable position, viz: the heavenly places in Christ Jesus, and we have to make the effort to be strong from that position. We have not to work up to that position, but to work *from* it with the full energy of will. It is impossible to live according to Our Lord's teaching without this secret of position. We do not get to the heavenly places by struggling, or aspiring, or consecration; God lifts us there, and if we will work from that position, He keeps us in His pavilion. No wonder the life of a saint appears such an unmitigated puzzle to rational human beings without the Spirit of God. It seems so ridiculous and so conceited to say that God Almighty is my Father and that He is looking after my affairs; but looked at from the position in which Jesus places us we find it is a marvellous revelation of truth.

"Set Upon a Rock"

Psalm 27: 5, 6

In our spiritual life God does not provide pinnacles on which we stand like spiritual acrobats; He provides tablelands of easy and delightful security. Recall the conception you had of holiness before you stood where you do to-day by the grace of God. It was the conception of a breathless standing on a pinnacle for a second at a time, but never with the thought of being able to live there. But when the Holy Spirit brought you there, you found it was not a pinnacle, but a plateau, a broad way, where the provision of strength and peace comes all the time, a place where it is much easier to live than lower down.

A Living Proposition

Romans 5: 12

"By one man sin entered into the world. . . ." The proposition that appeals to a healthy once-born man is that of self-realization— I want to develop myself. If you bring before him the proposition that he should be saved and give up his right to himself to Jesus Christ, it will be a dead proposition without meaning for him; but let conviction of sin, or disaster, or bereavement, or any of the great surprises of God touch him, and instantly the proposition takes on a totally new aspect and he will want to act on it. Jesus Christ always puts the emphasis on the effort of obedience, there must be a live quest of the will. "If you want to know My doctrine, i.e., whether it is of God or from Myself, *do My will*," says Jesus. The truth of God is only revealed to us by obedience.

The Cost of Cross-bearing

Matthew 10: 24

Jesus tells the disciples that they will be opposed not only in private life, but that the powers of state will oppose them and they will have to suffer persecution, and some even crucifixion. Do not say—But that was simply meant for those days. If you stand true to Jesus you will find that the world will react against you with a butt, not with a caress, annoyed and antagonistic (cf. John 15: 18-20).

When Our Lord spoke of the cross His disciples were to bear, He did not say that if they bore it they would become holy; He said the cross was to be borne for His sake, not for theirs. He also said that they would suffer in the same way as the prophet (Matt. 5: 11-12); they suffered because of the messages they spoke from God. The tendency to-day is to say—Live a holy life, but don't talk about it, don't give your testimony; don't confess your allegiance to Jesus, and you will be left alone.

The True Life of Faith

Hebrews 11: 8

It is not what a man achieves but what he believes and strives for that makes him noble and great. Hebrews 11 impresses this aspect of the life of faith over against the life of human perfection. The first thing faith in God does is to remove all thought of relevant perfection. Some lives may seem humanly perfect and yet not be relevant to God and His purpose. The effect such lives leave is not of a reach that exceeds its grasp, but of a completed little circle of their own. It takes a man completely severed from God to be perfect in that way. There is a difference between a perfect human life lived on earth and a personal life with God lived on earth; the former grasps that for which it reaches, the latter is grasped by that which it never can reach. The former chains us to earth by its very completeness; the latter causes us to fling ourselves unperplexed on God. The difference is not a question of sin, but the paradox of the incomplete perfection of a right relationship to God.

Enlarge Your Thinking
Philippians 4: 8

We are apt to discard the virtues of those who do not know Jesus Christ and call them pagan virtues. Paul says—If there is any virtue anywhere in the world, think about it, because the natural virtues are remnants of God's handiwork and will lead to the one central Source, Jesus Christ. We have to form the habit of keeping our mental life on the line of the great and beautiful things Paul mentions. It is not a prescribed ground. It is we who make limitations and then blame God for them. Many of us behave like ostriches, we put our heads in the sand and forget altogether about the world outside—"I have had this and that experience and I am not going to think of anything else." After a while we have aches and pains in the greater part of ourselves which is outside our heads, and then we find that God sanctifies every bit of us, spirit, soul and body. God grant we may get out into the larger horizons of God's Book.

The Goal of Perfection
Matthew 5: 48

Our Lord builds His deepest teaching on the instinct of emulation. When His Spirit comes in He makes me desire not to be inferior to Him Who called me. Our example is not a good man, not even a good Christian man, but God Himself. By the grace of God I have to emulate my Father in heaven. "Be ye therefore perfect, even as your Father which is in heaven is perfect" (Matt. 5: 48). The most natural instinct of the supernatural life of God within me is to be worthy of my Father. To say that the doctrine of sanctification is unnatural is not true; the doctrine is based on the way God has made us. When we are born again we become natural for the first time; as long as we are in sin we are abnormal, because sin is not normal.

Faithful Steward: Devoted Disciple

Genesis 24: 48; 1 Corinthians 4: 2

Eliezer in many respects stands as a picture of a disciple of the Lord, because the whole moulding of his life is his devotion to another, not to a sense of right or duty, but to his master (cf. John 13: 13-14). We know very little about devotion to Jesus Christ. We know devotion to right and to duty, but none of that is saintly, it is purely natural. The Sermon on the Mount nowhere tells us what our duty is; it tells us the things a saint will do—the things that are not his duty, e.g. Matt. 5: 39-42. Be renewed in the spirit of your mind, says Paul, not that you may do your duty, but that you may make out what God's will is.

All the reward Eliezer seeks is the happiness of his master; self-remembrance in him is dead. He is shrewd and practical yet as guileless as a child, the exact embodiment of 1 Cor. 4: 2—"It is required in stewards, that a man be found *faithful*."

Providence Recognized

Genesis 24: 58

Rebecca's brother and father recognize God's hand in the whole matter (v. 50), and Rebecca's consent is sought only on the point of departure. "And she said, I will go." Those words are the answer to Eliezer's prayer. Rebecca felt the thrill which always passes through any pure young heart in the presence of a saint. A soul's trust in a saint in the providence of God is something more precious even than love. Few of us know anything about it because we are too sordidly selfish; we want things for ourselves all the time. Eliezer had only one conception, loyalty to his master, and in the providence of God he brought Rebecca straight to Isaac. This marriage, like all true marriages, concerns the Kingdom of God.

Glorifying God in the Everyday

Matthew 5: 16

The wonder of the Incarnation slips into the Life of ordinary childhood; the marvel of the Transfiguration descends to the valley and the demon-possessed boy, and the glory of the Resurrection merges into Our Lord providing breakfast for His disciples on the sea shore in the early dawn. The tendency in early Christian experience is to look for the marvellous. We are apt to mistake the sense of the heroic for being heroes. It is one thing to go through a crisis grandly, but a different thing to go through every day glorifying God when there is no witness, no limelight, and no one paying the remotest attention to you. If we don't want medieval haloes, we want something that will make people say—What a wonderful man of prayer he is! What a pious, devoted woman she is! If anyone says that of you, you have not been loyal to God.

The Work of the God-Man

John 1: 14

Jesus Christ was not a Being who became Divine; He was the Godhead Incarnated. He emptied Himself of His glory in becoming Incarnate. Never separate the Incarnation from the Atonement. The Incarnation was not meant to enable God to realize Himself, but that man might realize God and gain readjustment to Him. Jesus Christ became Man for one purpose—that He might put away sin and bring the whole human race back into the oneness of identification. Jesus Christ is not an individual iota of a man; He is the whole of the human race centred before God in one Person: He is God and Man in one. Man is lifted up to God in Christ, and God is brought down to man in Christ. Jesus Christ nowhere said—He that hath seen *man* hath seen the Father; but He did say that God was manifest in human flesh in His own Person that He might become the generating centre for the same manifestation in every human being, and the place of His travail pangs is the Incarnation, Calvary, and the Resurrection.

Revelation Through Obedience

Genesis 22: 16–18

The promise of God stands in relation to Abraham's tried and willing obedience. The revelation of God to me is determined by my character, not by God's (Psalm 18: 25–26). If I am mean, that is how God will appear to me. "'Tis because I am mean, Thy ways so oft look mean to me." But by the discipline of obedience I come to the place Abraham reached and see God as He is. The promises of God are of no use to me until by obedience I understand the nature of God. We read some things in the Bible 365 times and they mean nothing to us, then all of a sudden we see what they mean, because in some particular we have obeyed God, and instantly His character is revealed. "For how many soever be the promises of God, in Him is the yea." The 'yea' must be born of obedience; when by the obedience of our life, we say "Amen," "So let it be," to a promise, then that promise is ours.

Blessing Through Sacrifice

Genesis 25: 7, 8

The more we have to sacrifice for God, the more glorious is the reward presently. We have no right to choose our sacrifice, God will let us see where the sacrifice is to come, and it will always be on the line of what God has given you, your 'Isaac,' and yet His call is to sacrifice it. God is always at work on the principle of lifting up the natural and making it and the spiritual one, and very few of us will go through with it. We will cling to the natural when God wants to put a sword through it. If you go through the transfiguration of the natural you will receive it back on a new plane altogether. God wants to make eternally our own what we only possessed intermittently.

The Cost of Christ-following

Luke 14: 33

To follow Jesus Christ to-day is to follow a madman according to the ideals of present day civilization. We have the idea that our civilization is God-ordained; but it has been built up by ourselves. We have made a thousand and one necessities until our system of civilized life is as cast iron, and then we apologize to the Lord for not following Him. "God can never mean that I have to follow Him at the cost of all I have?" But He does mean it. Instantly the clash is between our civilization and the call of Jesus Christ. Read the Sermon on the Mount—"Seek ye first the kingdom of God . . ." and apply it to modern life, and you will find its statements are either those of a madman or of God Incarnate.

Alone With the Divine Teacher

Mark 4: 34; John 16: 13, 14

Have you ever been alone with Jesus? The disciples enjoyed the inestimable privilege not only of hearing the truth from Our Lord's own lips, but of questioning Him in secret about everything He said. We go to John Wesley, or to Adam Clarke, or some other commentator instead of going to Jesus Himself. How can we go to Him? The Holy Spirit is the Exponent of Jesus Christ's statements, and He will test whether the expositions are of God or not. Jesus Christ's teaching is involved in such a manner that only the Holy Spirit can extricate its meaning for us. "He shall lead you into all truth." The Holy Spirit never witnesses to a clever interpretation; the exposition the Holy Spirit will witness to is always amazingly and profoundly simple.

The Divine Direction

Genesis 22: 3

God never fits His word to suit me; He fits me to suit His word. The discernment of God's call does not come in every moment of life but only in rare moments, the moments Our Lord spoke of as 'the light' (John 12: 35–36); we have to remain true to what we see in those moments, if we do not, we will put back God's purpose in our life. The undercurrent of regret in obeying the call of God arises from conferring with those who do not see with the one called, and if we listen to them we get into darkness. The life of Abraham is an illustration of two things: of unreserved surrender to God, and of God's complete possession of a child of His for His own highest ends.

The Duty of Diligence

Genesis 22: 3

"And Abraham rose up early in the morning."

This phrase is characteristic not only of men and women in the Bible but of God Himself. The revelation of God in the Old Testament is that of a working God. No other religion presents God either as diligent or as suffering, but as an all-in-all principle, ruling in lofty disdain. The God Who reveals Himself to Abraham is One ever intent on the fulfilment of His great designs; and like God, like people. If God is diligent, surely we ought to be diligent in doing our duty to Him. Think how patient and how diligent God has been with us! Over and over again God gets us near the point, and then by some petty individual sulk we spoil it all, and He patiently begins all over again. Think of the vision, 'whiter than snow shine,' God gave of what He wanted us to be—where has it gone? Has God had to begin all over again from where I left off last time, or have I said—I shall be true to God at all costs, no matter what the isolation?

Sacramental Discipleship

Galatians 6: 14

By the Cross of Christ I am saved from sin; by the Cross I am sanctified; but I never am a sacramental disciple until I deliberately lay myself on the altar of the Cross and give myself over emphatically and entirely to be actually what I am potentially in the sight of God, viz., a member of the Body of Christ. When I swing clear of myself and my own consciousness and give myself over to Jesus Christ, He can use me as a sacrament to nourish other lives.

Decrease and Increase

John 3: 30

Examine yourself in the light of these words. It is never that I drag God down into my sympathies, He lifts me clean into His. The more spiritually real I become, the less am I of any account, I become more and more of the nature of a grain of wheat falling into the earth and dying in order that it may bring forth fruit. "He must increase, but I must decrease." I only decrease as He increases, and He only increases in me as I nourish His life by that which decreases me. Am I willing to feed the life of the Son of God in me?

God's Will Overcoming in Us

1 John 4: 4

There is no such thing as fate; a human being always has the power to do the incalculable thing. There are fatal issues, but not fate. When God's decrees come to pass it is because men will not turn. God's will is supreme, but God never fights against us; it is self-will that fights against God. When the Spirit of God is at work in him a man lets God's will overcome. There is no fight, it is a higher power easily overcoming.

Is God Love?

1 John 4: 8

The love of God cannot make room for sin or self-interest, therefore the appeal of the love of God is not that of kindness and gentleness, but of holiness. If you take the natural view of the love of God you will become atheistic. If God were love according to our natural view of love He ought never to cause us pain, He ought to allow us to be peaceful; but the first thing God does is to cause us pain and to rouse us wide awake. That is why God looks cruel judged from the human sentimental standpoint; He loves us so much that He will not prevent us being hurt.

Sacramental Responsibility

Colossians 1: 24

By 'sacramental responsibility' understand the solemn determination to keep myself notably my Lord's, and to treat as a subtle temptation of the devil the call to take on any responsibility that conflicts with my determined identification with His interests. God's one great interest in men is that they are redeemed; am I identifying myself with that interest?

The Final Trust

Job 13: 15

Beware of everything that makes you pose religiously. A conscious pose springs from acquirements, not from vital life.

Experiences of what God has done for me are only stepping-stones; the one great note is—I trust in the Lord Jesus, God's providence can do with me what He likes, make the heavens like brass, earth like hell, my body loathsome—as Job's was; but the soul that is trusting in Jesus gets where Job got—"Though He slay me, yet will I trust in Him"—"I have no idea what God's purpose is, but I rest confidently in Him."

The Hidden Life

Matthew 6: 28

"Consider the lilies of the field, how they grow"—in the dark! We are apt to consider a lily when it is in the sunshine only, but for the greater part of the year it is buried in the ground. We imagine we are to be always above ground, shedding perfume and looking beautiful; or being continually cut and put into God's show room to be admired, forgetting altogether that we cannot grow and be cut at the same time. We cannot be as lilies unless we have spent time in the dark, totally ignored. Jesus says, as a disciple, consider your hidden life with God. When we breathe fresh air we are not consciously exhilaratingly different all the time; but if we continue to take in fresh air, it makes a profound difference. This is true of our life in Christ.

Spiritual Curiosity

1 Peter 2: 7

In natural life we grow by means of curiosity, and spiritually we grow by the same power. The Spirit of God uses the natural reaction of curiosity to enable us to know more about the One Who is precious. The instinct is not denied, but lifted on to a different platform and turned towards knowing Jesus Christ. As saints our curiosity must not be all abroad; Jesus Christ is the One Who rivets our attention, we become insatiably curious about Him. Think of the avidity with which you devour anything that has to do with expounding the Lord Jesus Christ. "Unto you therefore which believe He is precious."

His Cross and Ours

Luke 14: 27

The Cross of Christ stands unique and alone; we are never called upon to carry His Cross. Our cross is something that comes only with the peculiar relationship of a disciple to Jesus Christ, it is the evidence that we have denied the right to ourselves. The Cross of Jesus Christ is a revelation; our cross is an experience. Our Lord was not talking about suffering for conscience sake or conviction's sake; men suffer for conscience sake who know nothing about Jesus Christ and owe Him no allegiance; men suffer for conviction's sake if they are worth their salt, whether they are Christians or not.

What the Cross was to our Lord such also in measure was it to be to those who followed Him. The Cross is the pain involved in doing the will of God.

Bane and Blessing in the Cross

Matthew 10: 22, 24, 25

These verses need to be re-read because we are apt to think that Jesus Christ took all the bitterness, and we get all the blessing. It is true that we get the blessing, but we must never forget that the wine of life is made out of crushed grapes; to follow Him will involve bruising in the lives of the disciples as the purpose of God did in His own life. The thing that makes us whimper is that we will look for justice. If in your Christian work you look for justice you will soon put yourself in a bandage and give way to self-pity and discouragement. Never look for justice, but never cease to give it; and never allow anything you meet with to sour your relationship to men through Jesus Christ. "Love as I have loved you."

Preaching the Cross With Passion

1 Corinthians 1: 23

Never confuse the Cross of Christ with the benefits that flow from it. For all his doctrine, Paul's one great passion was the Cross of Christ, not salvation, nor sanctification, but the great truth that God so loved the world that He gave His only begotten Son; consequently you never find Paul artificial, or making a feeble statement. Every doctrine he taught had the blood and the power of God in it. There is an amazing force of spirit in all he said because the great passion behind it was not that he wanted men to be holy, that was secondary, but that he had come to understand what God meant by the Cross of Christ. If I have the idea of personal holiness only, of being put in God's showroom, I will never come anywhere near seeing what God wants; but when once I have come where Paul is, and God is enabling me to understand what the Cross of Christ means, then nothing can ever turn me.

Preaching the Crucified With Passion

1 Corinthians 2: 2

You cannot be profoundly moved by a sentiment or by an idea of holiness, but you can be moved by a passion; and the old writers used to speak of the Cross as the Passion of Our Lord. The one impression left by Paul, whether his words were stinging or comforting, for praise or for condemnation, was Christ and Him crucified, not risen and exalted, but *crucified*. The reason some of us have no power, no sense of awe, in our preaching, is that we have no passion for God, only a passion for Humanity. The one thing we have to do is to exhibit Jesus Christ crucified, to lift Him up all the time and "I, if I be lifted up, will draw all men unto Me." Paul had one passion only, he had seen the light of the knowledge of the glory of God in the face of Jesus Christ. Who is Jesus Christ? God exalted in Christ crucified.

The Cross, a Stumbling Block

1 Corinthians 1: 23

There is no such thing as *sin* to intellectual reasoning, and consequently no meaning in the Cross, because that point of view rules out what the Bible bases everything on. The Bible bases everything on the hiatus produced by sin between God and man, as well as on the Cross where Jesus Christ deals with sin. When intellectual reasoning comes to the Cross it is embarrassed because it looks on the Cross as the death of a martyr, one who lived beyond his dispensation. According to the New Testament the Cross is not the death of a man, it is the Cross of God.

The Grape and the Wine

John 15: 8

If you want to remain a full-orbed grape you must keep out of God's hands for He will crush you; wine cannot be had in any other way. The curse in Christian work is that we want to preserve ourselves in God's museum; what God wants is to see where Jesus Christ's men and women are. The saints are always amongst the unofficial crowd, the crowd that is not noticed, and their one dominant note is Jesus Christ.

God's Heart Revealed

Matthew 27: 46

The Cross is the crystallized point in history where Eternity merges with Time. The cry on the Cross, "My God, My God, why hast Thou forsaken Me?" is not the desolation of an isolated individual: it is the revelation of the heart of God face to face with the sin of man, and going deeper down than man's sin can ever go in inconceivable heartbreak in order that every sin-stained, hell-deserving sinner might be absolutely redeemed.

Propitiation Through the Cross

1 John 2: 2

If the significance of Christ as the propitiation is immense, the domain to which His propitiation applies is limitless also. Sinfulness against Christ is as limitless as the propitiation. . . . We are not to talk sentimental nonsense about the Universal Fatherhood of God; to knock the bottom board out of Redemption by saying that God is love and of course He will forgive sin. . . . The only ground on which God can forgive sin and reinstate us in His favour, is through the Cross of Christ, and in no other way.

The Cleansing Blood

1 John 1: 7

When we speak of the blood of Jesus Christ cleansing us from all sin, we do not mean the physical blood shed on Calvary, but the whole life of the Son of God which was poured out to redeem the world. All the perfections of the essential nature of God were in that blood, and all the holiest attainments of mankind as well. It was the life of the perfection of Deity that was poured out on Calvary, . . .

The Wonder of Redemption

John 1: 29

God Almighty took the problem of the sin of the world on His own shoulders, and it made Him stoop; He rehabilitated the whole human race, that is, He put the human race back where He designed it to be, and any one of us in our actual conditions can enter into union with God on the ground of Jesus Christ's Redemption. . . . A man cannot redeem himself; Redemption is absolutely finished and complete; its reference to individual men is a question of their individual action.

Thinking God's Thoughts

Isaiah 55: 8

As soon as we begin to examine the foundations of our salvation we are up against the thoughts of God, and as Christians we ought to be busy thinking God's thoughts after Him. That is where we fall short to-day, we are delighted with the fact that "Once I was this, and now I am that," but simply to have a vivid experience is not sufficient if we are to be at our best for God. It is because Christians have refused to think on Christian lines that Satan has come in as an angel of light and switched off numbers of God's children in their heads, with the result that there is a divorce between heart and head.

God in the Commonplace

1 Kings 19: 11, 12

The ministrations of God come over and over again in the most commonplace manner possible. We look for some great big alteration, something marvellous like the wind, or an earthquake, or fire; and the voice of God tells us to do what the most ordinary voice we know might tell us to do. "And after the fire a still small voice"—i.e., "a sound of gentle stillness"—the one thing the Lord was in.

The Revealing Crisis
Luke 9: 62

Over and over again men and women who should stand in the forefront for God are knocked clean out when a crisis comes, the reason is not external wrongdoing, but there is something in which Jesus Christ has not had His right of way, something has never been given up, and their discipleship is marred. God gives us ample opportunity of proving whether we have really given up the right to ourselves to Jesus Christ. The one who has offers no hindrance to the Holy Spirit working through him.

Baffled!
Job 3: 20-26

The experience of being baffled is common to us all, and the more religious and thoughtful a man is, the more intensely is he baffled. With regard to your own baffling, recognize it and state it, but don't state it dishonestly to yourself. Don't say you are not baffled if you are, and don't tell a lie in order to justify your belief in God. If you are in the dark, don't take refuge in any subterfuge which you know is not true. Never take an answer that satisfies your mind only; insist on an answer that satisfies more than your mind.

April 4th

Wind, Earthquake and Fire

1 Kings 19: 11, 12

To-day there are colossal forces abroad and God is using them as His instruments, but He is not 'in' them, that is, they are not God. It is a misconception to imagine that God is bound up in His instruments; He uses forces and powers for His own ends, but they must never be mistaken for Himself. An instrument conveys God's message, and a man used by God ought to be a holy man: but it does not always follow that he is (cf. Matt. 7: 21, 22).

April 5th

'In Adam' or 'In Christ'

1 Corinthians 15: 22

The terms 'in Adam,' 'in Christ,' are not mystical terms, but actual revelations of man's condition. When we are 'in Adam' we get down to the desolating desert aspect of life. Take love—the most abiding thing about love is its tragedy; or life, the most desolating thing about life is its climax, death. When we are 'in Christ' the whole thing is reversed. We read that "Jesus advanced in wisdom and stature and in favour with God and men"—He never ate of the fruit of the tree of good and evil, He knew evil only by contrast with good. When a man is born from above the desolating desert aspect of life goes. There is no sadness now in natural love, it ends nowhere but in the heart of God; 'in Christ' life knows no death, it goes on more and more fully. If you want to know God's original design for man, you see it in Jesus Christ; He was easily Master of the life on the earth, in the air and in the sea, not as God, but as Man; it was the human in Jesus that was master.

The Door of Destitution

Matthew 5: 3

Our Lord begins where we would never begin, at the point of human destitution. The greatest blessing a man ever gets from God is the realization that if he is going to enter into His Kingdom it must be through the door of destitution. Naturally we do not want to begin there, that is why the appeal of Jesus is of no use until we come face to face with realities; then the only One worth listening to is the Lord. We learn to welcome the patience of Jesus only when we get to the point of human destitution. It is not that God *will not* do anything for us until we get there, but that He *cannot*. God can do nothing for me if I am sufficient for myself. When we come to the place of destitution spiritually we find the Lord waiting, and saying, "If any man thirst, let him come unto Me, and drink."

The Bank of Faith

John 20: 29

Seeing is never believing: we interpret what we see in the light of what we believe. Faith is confidence in God before you see God emerging, therefore the nature of faith is that it must be tried. To say "Oh yes, I believe God will triumph" may be so much credence smeared over with religious phraseology; but when you are up against things it is quite another matter to say, "I believe God will win through." The trial of our faith gives us a good banking account in the heavenly places, and when the next trial comes our wealth there will tide us over. If we have confidence in God beyond the actual earthly horizons, we shall see the lie at the heart of the fear, and our faith will win through in every detail. Jesus said that men ought always to pray and not 'cave in'—"Don't look at the immediate horizon and don't take the facts you see and say they are the reality; they are actuality; the Reality lies behind with God."

"Having Done All To Stand"

Ephesians 6: 11-20

Paul is writing from prison; he knows all about the Roman soldier whose armour he is describing, for he was chained to one of them. "I am an ambassador in a chain," he says.

These verses are not a picture of how to fight, but of how not to fight. If you have not put on the armour, you will have to fight; but "having put on the whole armour of God," says Paul, "then *stand*." There are times when God's servants are sent out to attack, to storm the citadel, but the counsel given here is as to how we are to hold the position which has been gained. We need to learn this conservation of energy, "having done all, to stand," manifesting the full power of God.

Hard Words

Mark 10: 26

Jesus Christ says a great deal that we listen to, but we do not hear it. When we *do* hear, His words are amazingly hard. These words were so hard that His very disciples were staggered—"And they that heard it said, Who then can be saved?" (v. 26). Jesus did not seem the least solicitous that the rich young ruler should do what He told him, He made no attempt to keep him with Him, He simply said—"Sell all that thou hast, . . . and come, follow me."

Deliberate Detachment

Matthew 19: 21

"Sell all that thou hast and distribute unto the poor." There is a general principle here and a particular reference. We are always in danger of taking the particular reference for the general principle and evading the general principle. The particular reference here is to selling material goods. The rich young ruler had deliberately to be destitute, deliberately to distribute, deliberately to discern where his treasure was, and to devote himself to Jesus Christ. The principle underlying it is that I must detach myself from everything I possess.

Spiritual Concentration

Daniel 9: 3

"And I set my face . . ."

We discern spiritual truth not by intellectual curiosity or research, but by entreating the favour of the Lord, that is, by prayer and by no other way, not even by obedience, because obedience is apt to have an idea of merit. If we are not concentrated we affect a great many attitudes; but when we 'set our faces unto the Lord God' all affectation is gone—the religious pose, the devout pose, the pious pose, all go instantly when we determine to concentrate; our attention is so concentrated that we have no time to wonder how we look. "This one thing I do . . ." says Paul; his whole attention was fixed on God. Is my mind fixed entirely on God, or on service for God?

The Spirit Here to Be Received

Luke 11: 13

We are told by some that it is foolish to ask God for the Holy Spirit because this is the dispensation of the Holy Spirit. Thank God it is! God's mighty Spirit is with all men, He impinges on men's lives at all points and in unexpected places; but the great need is to receive the Holy Spirit that He may do *in* us all that Jesus Christ did *for* us on the Cross. There stands the mighty charter for every man and woman who will put it to the test—"If ye then, being evil, know how to give good gifts unto your children: how much more shall your Heavenly Father give the Holy Spirit to them that ask Him?" (Luke 11: 13).

The regenerating and sanctifying work of the Holy Spirit is to incorporate us into Christ until we are living witnesses to Him.

Submitting to His Word and Will

John 8: 28

The secret of Our Lord's holy speech was that He habitually submitted His intelligence to His Father. When ever problems pressed on the human side, as they did in the temptation, Our Lord had within Himself the Divine remembrance that every problem had been solved in counsel with His Father before He became Incarnate (cf. Rev. 13: 8), and that therefore the one thing for Him was to do the will of His Father, and to do it His Father's way. Satan tried to hasten Him, tried to make Him face the problems as a Man and do God's will in His own way: "The Son can do nothing of himself, but what he seeth the Father doing."

Are we intellectually insubordinate, spiritually stiff-necked, dictating to God in pious phraseology what we intend to let Him make us, hunting through the Bible to back up our pet theories? Or have we learned the secret of submitting our intelligence and our reasoning to Jesus Christ's word and will as He submitted His mind to His Father?

'In the Form of a Servant'

Philippians 2: 7

". . . *taking the form of a servant.*" Our Lord took upon Him habitually the part of a slave: "I am among you as he that serveth." Consequently He could be 'put upon' to any extent, unless His Father prevented it (cf. John 19: 11) or His Father's honour was at stake (cf. Mark 11: 15-19). It was our Lord's right to be 'in the form of God', but He renounced that right and took 'the form of a bond-servant,' not the form of a nobleman but of a slave. Our Lord crowned the words that the powers of this world detest—'servant,' 'obedience,' 'humility,' 'service.'

The Divine Self-emptying

Philippians 2: 7 (R.V.)

". . . *but emptied himself.*" Jesus Christ effaced the Godhead in Himself so effectually that men without the Spirit of God despised Him. No one without the Spirit of God, or apart from a sudden revelation from God, ever saw the true self of Jesus whilst He was on earth. He was 'as a root out of a dry ground,' thoroughly disadvantaged in the eyes of everyone not convicted of sin. The reference in 2 Cor. 8: 9 is not to a wealthy *man* becoming poor, but to a wealthy *God* becoming poor for men. The purpose of the Incarnation was to remove sin from human nature. To those who seek after wisdom the preaching of Christ crucified is foolishness; but when a man knows that his life is twisted, that the mainspring is wrong, he is in the state of heart and mind to understand why it was necessary for God to become Incarnate. The doctrine of the Self-limitation of Jesus is clear to our hearts first, not to our heads. We cannot form the mind of Christ unless we have His Spirit, nor can we understand Our Lord's teaching apart from His Spirit. We cannot see through it; but when once we receive His Spirit we know implicitly what He means.

"Obedient Unto Death"

Philippians 2: 8 (R.V.)

. . . *"and being found in fashion as a man, he humbled himself, becoming obedient even unto death, yea, the death of the cross."* Right at the threshold of His manhood Our Lord took upon Him His vocation, which was to bear away the sin of the world—by *identification*, not by sympathy (John 1: 29). Our Lord's object in becoming Deity Incarnate was to redeem mankind, and Satan's final onslaught in the Garden of Gethsemane was against Our Lord *as Son of Man*, viz.: that the purpose of His Incarnation would fail. The profundity of His agony has to do with the fulfilling of His destiny. The Cross is a triumph for *the Son of Man*; any and every man has freedom of access straight to the throne of God by right of what Our Lord accomplished through His death on the Cross.

Habit Forming . . . Character Building

2 Peter 1: 5-7

Always distinguish between the defects of a growing life and the vices of a mature life. Be as merciless as God can make you with the vices of a mature life, but be endlessly patient with the defects of a growing life. A young life is always in chaos, but there is one main trend coming out all the time, and that trend can be garrisoned by intercessory prayer.

God never makes character; God puts into us the disposition of His Son, and on that basis we have to form character. As we form the habit of doing things in accordance with the disposition of Jesus Christ we are backed by inward supplies of God's grace. Every habit begins with difficulty. Habit is a mechanical process of which we have ceased to become conscious. A man who is right with God does the right thing instinctively. "Add to your faith virtue. . . ." These things do not emerge until we so form the habit of doing them that they become characteristic of our lives.

April 18th

His Love Gift to God, and Ours

John 17: 19

If we have entered into the experience of sanctification, what are we doing with our holy selves? Do we every morning we waken thank God that we have a self to give to Him, a self that He has purified and adjusted and baptized with the Holy Ghost so that we might sacrifice it to Him? Sacrifice in its essence is the exuberant passionate love-gift of the best I have to the one I love best. The best gift the Son of God had was His holy Manhood, and He gave that as a love-gift to God that He might use it as an Atonement for the world. "He poured out his soul unto death," and that is to be the characteristic of our lives. God is at perfect liberty to waste us if He chooses. We are sanctified for one purpose only, that we might sanctify our sanctification and give it to God.

April 19th

Circumstances, Dark and Bright

Romans 8: 28

Never confound circumstances with environment. Environment is the element in our circumstances that fits our disposition. We cannot control our circumstances, but we are the deciders of our own environment. We have to remember the 'altogetherness' of circumstances (cf. Romans 8: 28). If your circumstances are dark blue just now, remember the time when they were bright pink. It is not the dark blue circumstances or the bright pink circumstances that work for good, but the 'togetherness' of them that works for good. Circumstances either produce energy and smeddum (i.e. grit, courage and pluck) or enervation. The marvellous thing about the life of God in us is that there is no reaction of exhaustion, but a continual pouring in all the time (Psalm 87: 7). If we work from the real source of energy, viz. our relationship to God, everything that happens brings more life and fuller, with no reaction.

Enjoying the Disagreeable
Philippians 4: 12, 13

It is one thing to go into the disagreeable by God's engineering, but another thing to go into it by choice. If God puts us there He is amply sufficient. No matter how difficult the circumstances may be, if we will let Jesus Christ manifest Himself in them, it will prove to be a new means of exhibiting the wonderful perfection and extraordinary purity of the Son of God. This keen enthusiasm of letting the Son of God manifest Himself in us is the only thing that will keep us enjoying the disagreeable.

The Joy and Peace of the Satisfied
Ephesians 2: 5, 6

If all Jesus Christ came to do was to upset me, make me unfit for my work, upset my friendships and my life, produce disturbance and misery and distress, then I wish He had never come. But that is not all He came to do. He came to lift us up into the heavenly places where He is Himself. The whole claim of the Redemption of Jesus Christ is that He can satisfy the last aching abyss of the human soul, not hereafter only, but here and now. Satisfaction does not mean stagnation, it means the knowledge that we have the right type of life for our souls. The phrase in the hymn, "Oh the peace my Saviour gives," is a Biblical one. That peace is the deepest thing a human personality can know, it is almighty. The Apostle Paul emphasizes the hilarity of life. "Be not drunk with wine, . . . but be filled with the Spirit." Enthusiasm is the idea, intoxicated with the life of God Psalm 73 is a description of the bad man having all that heart can desire; that is satisfaction without God. A bad man has a hilarious time, and a man whose life is right has a hilarious time. The healthy pagan and the healthy saint are the ones described in God's Book as hilarious; all in between are diseased and more or less sick.

The Worldling and the Christian

Luke 12: 19

Never have the idea that a worldling is unhappy—a worldling is perfectly happy, as thoroughly happy as a Christian. The persons who are unhappy are the worldlings or the Christians if they are not at one with the principle that binds them. When a worldling is not a worldling at heart, he is miserable; and when a Christian is not a Christian at heart, he is miserable, he carries his religion like a headache instead of something that is worth having. A worldling is one who has wisely kept within bounds of the disposition which the Bible alone reveals as the disposition of sin, viz., my claim to my right to myself. When once that is broken into by overt acts of wrongdoing, the worldling is miserable, and he ceases to be a true worldling. Remember, then, the two things that disintegrate the devil's kingdom—breaking out into acts of sin and the conviction of the Spirit of God. This is the solution of a number of moral problems.

Here for One Thing Only

2 Corinthians 5: 9 (R.V.)

"I am here for one thing only, for Jesus Christ to manifest Himself in me." That is to be the steadfast habit of a Christian's life. Whenever we think we are of use to God, we hinder Him. We have to form the habit of letting God carry on His work through us without let or hindrance as He did through Jesus, and He will use us in ways He dare not let us see. We have to efface every other thought but that of Jesus Christ; it is not done once for all; we have to be always doing it. If once you have seen that Jesus Christ is all in all, make the habit of letting Him be all in all. It will mean that you not only have implicit faith that He is all in all, but that you go through the trial of your faith and prove that He is. After sanctification God delights to put us into places where He can make us wealthy.

The Witness of the Spirit-filled Life

Acts 4: 13

"We have the Bible bound in morocco, bound in all kinds of beautiful leather. What we need is the Bible bound in shoe leather." That is exactly the teaching of Our Lord. After the disciples had received the Holy Spirit they became witnesses to Jesus, their lives spoke more eloquently than their lips—"and they took knowledge of them, that they had been with Jesus." The Holy Spirit being imparted to us and expressed through us is the manifested exhibition that God can do all that His Book states He can. It is those who have received the Holy Spirit who understand the will of God and "grow up into Him in all things." When the Scriptures are made quick and powerful by the Holy Spirit, they fit every need of life.

The Peril of Impulse

John 16: 13, 14

Any impulse which does not lead to the glorification of Jesus Christ has the snare of Satan behind it. People say, "How am I to know whether my impulse is from the Holy Spirit or from my own imagination?" Very easily. Jesus Christ gave us the simplest, most easy-to-be-understood tests for guidance—"The Holy Ghost . . . shall teach you all things, and shall bring all things to your remembrance, whatsoever I have said unto you;" the Holy Spirit "will guide you into all truth: for He shall not speak of Himself." Beware of any religious experience which glorifies you and not Jesus Christ.

The Crown and the Cross

Luke 9: 29; Hebrews 2: 9

We say, "No cross, no crown;" in the life of Our Lord the crown of the glory of the Transfiguration came before the Cross. You never know Jesus Christ, and Him crucified, unless you have seen Him transfigured in all His transcendent majesty and glory; the Cross to you is nothing but the cross of a martyr. If you have seen Jesus glorified, you know that the Cross is the revelation of God's judgment on sin, that on the Cross Our Lord bore the whole massed sin of the human race. "Him Who knew no sin He made to be sin on our behalf." No wonder we say:

> Since mine eyes have looked on Jesus
> I've lost sight of all beside.

Have we seen Him, "crowned with glory and honour"?

Be Spiritually Tenacious

Revelation 3: 10

One of the greatest strains in life is the strain of waiting for God. "Because thou didst keep the word of My patience." God takes the saints like a bow which He stretches and at a certain point the saint says, "I can't stand any more," but God does not heed, He goes on stretching because He is aiming at His mark, not ours, and the patience of the saints is that they 'hang in' until God lets the arrow fly.

If your hopes are being disappointed just now it means that they are being purified. There is nothing noble the human mind has ever hoped for or dreamed of that will not be fulfilled. Don't jump to conclusions too quickly; one or two things lie unsolved, and the biggest test of all is that God looks as if He were totally indifferent.

April 28th
Partakers of His Holiness
Hebrews 12: 10

The characteristic of the holiness of Almighty God is that it is absolute, it is impossible to antagonize or strain it. The characteristic of the holiness of Jesus is that it manifested itself by means of antagonism, it was a holiness that could be tested (*see* Hebrews 4: 15). The Son of God, as Son of Man, transformed innocence into holy character bit by bit as things opposed; He did not exhibit an immutable holiness but a holiness of which we can be made partakers—"that we might be partakers of His holiness" (Hebrews 12: 10). Jesus Christ revealed what a normal man should be and in so doing showed how we may become all that God wants us to be.

April 29th
Do Not Panic
Matthew 24: 6

That is either the statement of a madman or of a Being who has power to put something into a man and keep him free from panic, even in the midst of the awful terror of war. The basis of panic is always cowardice. Our Lord teaches us to look things full in the face. He says—"When you hear of wars, don't be scared." It is the most natural thing in the world to be scared, and the clearest evidence that God's grace is at work in our hearts is when we do not get into panics. Our Lord insists on the inevitableness of peril. He says, "You must lay your account with war, with hatred, and with death."

God's Hidden Purpose

Mark 6: 45-52

There was no point of rest for the natural minds of the disciples as to what Jesus was after—it was the deep, the dark, and the dreadful. Our Lord's purpose was that they should see Him walking on the sea. We have an idea that God is leading us to a certain goal, a desired haven; He is not. The question of getting to a particular end is a mere incident. "For I know the plans that I am planning for you, saith the Lord, plans of welfare, and not of calamity, to give you end and expectation" (Jeremiah 29: 11). What men call the process, God calls the end. If you can stay in the midst of the turmoil unperplexed and calm because you see Jesus, that is God's purpose in your life; not that you may be able to say "I have done this and that and now it's all right." God's purpose for you is that you depend upon Him and His power *now*; that you see Him walking on the waves—no shore in sight, no success, just the absolute certainty that it is all right because you see Him.

"Silent Unto God"

Psalm 62: 5 (R.V. margin)

"My soul, be silent unto God." Rouse your soul out of its drowsiness to consider God. Fix your attention on God, on the great themes of His Redemption and His holiness, on the great and glorious outlines of His character, be silent to Him there; then be as busy as you like in the ordinary affairs of life. Be like the Lord Jesus; when He was sound asleep in the fishing-boat He knew that His Father would waken Him when He wanted Him. This is a marvellous picture of confidence in God.

The Blessing of Ownership

1 Corinthians 3: 23

The Spirit of God brings us into the realization of our ownership, and the instinct of ownership becomes a tremendous wealth in the life. "All things are yours." Paul prays that the eyes of our understanding may be enlightened that we may know what is ours in Christ Jesus.

No personality, from the tiniest child to Almighty God, is without this sense of ownership. How wonderfully sprightly a dog looks when he is owned! How weary and hangdog we become when we are convicted of sin; but when we experience God's salvation, we straighten up immediately, everything is altered, we can fling our heads back and look the world in the face because the Lord is ours and we are His. A dominant ownership, such as the Lord's, means that we own everything He owns. "The meek shall inherit the earth."

The Deepest Longing

Philippians 3: 8-12

You are getting tired of life as it is, tired of yourself as you are, getting sour with regard to the setting of your life; lift your eyes for one moment to Jesus Christ. Do you want, more than you want your food, more than you want your sleep, more than you want anything under heaven, or in heaven, that Jesus Christ might so identify you with Himself that you are His first and last and for ever? God grant that the great longing desire of your heart may begin to awaken as it has never done, not only the desire for the forgiveness of sin, but for identification with Jesus Himself until you say, "I live, yet not I, but Christ liveth in me."

Faith in the Great Redemption
John 19: 30

We can never expound the Redemption, but we must have strong unshaken faith in it so that we art not swept off our feet by actual things. That the devil and man are allowed to do as they like is a mere episode in the providence of God. Everything that has been touched by sin and the devil has been redeemed; we are to live in the world immovably banked in that faith. Unless we have faith in the Redemption, all our activities are fussy impertinences which tell God He is doing nothing. We destroy our souls serving Jesus Christ, instead of abiding in Him. Jesus Christ is not working out the Redemption, it is complete; we are working it out, and beginning to realize it by obedience. Our practical life is to be moulded by our belief in the Redemption, and our declared message will be in accordance with our belief. If we say we believe "It is finished" we must not blaspheme God by unbelief in any domain of our practical life.

The Frontiers of Death
John 6: 53

This is not a sad statement, but a joyful one. Whenever we think we can get the life of God by obedience or prayer or some kind of discipline, we are wrong. We must realize the frontiers of death, that there is no more chance of our entering into the life of God than a mineral has of entering the vegetable kingdom; we can only enter into the Kingdom of God if God will stoop down and lift us up. That is exactly what Jesus Christ promises to do. The bedrock of spiritual life as our Lord taught is poverty—"Blessed are the poor in spirit," not, "Blessed are the strong-willed, or the prayerful or the consecrated," but, "Blessed is the man who knows he is weak." When we get there the surprise of God's life may come at any time.

May 6th

The Springs of Love

John 17: 26

The springs of love are in God; that means love cannot be found anywhere else. It is absurd for us to try and find the love of God in our hearts naturally, it is not there any more than the life of Jesus Christ is there. Love and life are in God and in Jesus Christ and in the Holy Spirit Whom God gives to us, not because we merit Him, but according to His own particular graciousness. We cannot say in the abstract, "I am going to love my enemies," because naturally we hate them; but when we have a real actual enemy if the love of God is in us, we find we do not hate him. The point is that the springs of love are in the Holy Spirit, not in us. We cannot order the Holy Spirit to come into us; we believe in God, He does the rest.

May 7th

Willing Poverty for God

2 Corinthians 8: 9

To be willingly poor for God is to strip myself of all things for the sake of Jesus Christ. One of the greatest snares is built on what is really a great truth, viz., that every man has Christ in himself. The pernicious use that is made of that statement is that therefore man draws power from himself. Never! Jesus Christ never drew power from Himself: He drew it always from without Himself, viz., from His Father. "The Son can do nothing of Himself" (John 5: 19 and 30). Beware of being rich spiritually on earth, only be rich spiritually in heaven. Jesus said to the rich young ruler, "If you will strip yourself and have no riches here, you will lay up for yourself treasure in heaven." Treasure in heaven is faith that has been tried (cf. Revelation 3: 18). Immediately we begin to have fellowship with Jesus we have to live the life of faith at all costs; it may be bitter to begin with, but afterwards it is ineffably and indescribably sweet —willing poverty for God, a determined going outside myself and every earthly thing.

The 'If' of Discipleship

Luke 14: 26, 27

Jesus Christ always talked about discipleship with an 'If.' We are at perfect liberty to toss our spiritual head and say, "No thank you, that is a bit too stern for me," and the Lord will never say a word, we can do exactly what we like; He will never plead, but the opportunity is there, 'If . . .'

After all, it is the great stern call of Jesus that fascinates men and women quicker than anything. It is not the gospel of being saved from hell and enjoying heaven that attracts men, saving in a very shallow mood; it is Christ crucified that attracts men; Jesus said so —"I, if I be lifted up from the earth, will draw all men unto Me." Jesus Christ never attracts us by the unspeakable bliss of Paradise; He attracts us by an ugly beam.

Confession of the Childlike Attitude

Jeremiah 10: 23

"Lord, I know that the way of man is not in himself: it is not in man that walketh to direct his steps"—is a confession, not of sin, but of realized condition. Have we ever made that confession in our own souls before God? If we have, we know, and delight to know, that it is not within man's power to arrange the course of his life. The test is, have we the childlike attitude towards God, are we always on the look-out for His supernatural working? Most of us are rationalistic infidels, we never think that God is supernatural at all. We rule out the miraculous and the supernatural because it is not according to the outlook of to-day.

Willing for the Loss of All Things?

Philippians 3: 7, 8

". . . for Whom I suffered the loss of all things." To experience the loss of all things for anyone but Jesus Christ is mental suicide. Read what Our Lord said to the rich young ruler—"Sell whatsoever thou hast, . . . and come, follow Me"—"Reduce yourself until you are a mere conscious man, and then give that manhood to Me;" and we read that "his countenance fell at the saying, and he went away sorrowful: for he was one that had great possessions." Do you possess a reputation as a Christian worker? That will be in the way when the Lord speaks to you. Are you rich in the consciousness that you are somebody spiritually? That will be in the way. You must first estimate and then experience the loss of all things and cast yourself on Jesus, then participation in godliness will be yours as it never has been.

Intellectual Intemperance

James 1: 22

Intellectual intemperance is a great snare to a saint. Bodily fasting is child's play compared to the determined fasting from the intellectual apprehension of the teachings of Jesus that goes beyond what we are living out. The characteristic of many spiritual people to-day is intellectual intemperance, fanatical intoxication with the things of God, wild exuberance, an unlikeness to the sanity of Jesus in the very ways of God. There is a danger in the enjoyment of the delights and the power that come to us through Jesus Christ's salvation without lifting the life into keeping with His teaching, especially in spiritual people whose minds have never been disciplined and they wander off into all kinds of vagaries. That accounts for the distinction we find between spiritual sincerity and spiritual reality.

May 12th

The Central Citadel for God

Psalm 144: 2; Isaiah 50: 10

Watch the hard things Jesus says about father, mother, wife, children, our own life (*see* Luke 14: 26); He says if we are going to follow Him, these must be on the outside of the central citadel. The central citadel must be God and God alone. When once we are willing to 'do to death' our clinging to creatures, which in certain supreme calls comes between ourselves and God, Jesus says we will receive a hundredfold, because immediately we are rightly related to God He can trust us with creature-relationships without fear of inordinateness.

May 13th

Is the Cross an Offence?

1 Corinthians 1: 18–23

Remember, it was not the 'offscouring' that crucified Jesus, it was the highest reach of natural morality crucified Him. It is the refined, cultured, religious, moral people who refuse to sacrifice the natural for the spiritual. When once you get that thought, you understand the inveterate detestation of the Cross of Christ. Where are we with regard to this barter? Are we disciples of Jesus? Who is first, or what is first, in our lives? Who is the dominating personality that is dearer to us than life, ourselves or someone else? If it is someone else, who is it? It is only on such lines as these that we come to understand what Jesus meant when He said, "If any man would come after Me, let him deny himself." What He means is that He and what He stands for must be first.

Salvation Expressed in Bodily Life

Romans 6: 19

Paul is strong in urging us to realize what salvation means in our bodily lives; it means that we command our bodies to obey the new disposition. That is where you find the problems on the margins of the sanctified life. Paul argues in Romans 6: 19, "You are perfectly adjusted to God on the inside by a perfect Saviour, but your members have been used as servants of the wrong disposition; now begin to make those same members obey the new disposition." As we go on, we find every place God brings us into is the means of enabling us to realize with growing joy that the life of Christ within is more than a match, not only for the enemy on the outside, but for the impaired body that comes between. Paul urges with passionate pleading, that we present our bodies a living sacrifice, and then realize, not presumptuously, but with slow, sure, overwhelming certainty that every command of Christ can be obeyed in our bodily life through the Atonement.

Only God Understands Us

Psalm 139: 1-3

As long as we think we understand ourselves we are in a lamentable state of ignorance. The first dose of conviction of sin, or of the realization of what the Psalmist states—the unfathomable depths of our own souls—will put an end to that ignorance. The only One Who can redeem the human soul is the Lord Jesus Christ, and He has done it, and the Holy Spirit brings the realization of this to us experimentally. All this vast complex 'me' which we cannot begin to understand, God knows completely, and through the Atonement He invades every part of our personality with His life. There is nothing simple in the human soul or in human life. The only simple thing is the relationship of the soul to Jesus Christ, and Paul says he fears lest we should be corrupted from that simplicity (2 Cor. 11: 3).

The Secret of True Fellowship
Acts 2: 42; Hebrews 10: 24, 25

These passages indicate the main characteristic of Christianity in its working out, viz., the 'together' aspect. Our Lord never inculcated an isolated holy life. Immediately we fix our eyes on our own whiteness, we lose sight of the purpose of Christianity. The Holy Spirit within a man makes him fix his eyes on his Lord, and on intense activity for other people. The individual man becomes so interdependent that he slowly loses his self-assertiveness until the oneness Jesus Christ prayed for is fulfilled. "If we walk in the light as God is in the light, . . . we have fellowship one with another." The Holy Spirit entering into the personal spirit instantly puts us into affinity with every other person in the light, hence Christian fellowship. Christian fellowship has nothing to do with individual affinities, which are merely the husk of personality.

The Gospel Creates Resentment
Romans 8: 7

The Gospel does not present what the natural man wants, but what he needs, and the Gospel awakens an intense resentment as well as an intense craving. Why should the thing that upsets my peace be preached? I am living a simple, healthy, pagan life, my life does not spit through my creed and ridicule me, why should I be faced with an ideal which makes me know how tantalizingly short I come of it? At first the Gospel instead of being attractive is the opposite. The natural heart does not want the Gospel. We will take God's blessings and lovingkindnesses, but when it comes to the need of having the disposition of my soul altered, we find there is opposition at once. When we come down to close quarters and God's Spirit tells us we must give up the right to ourselves to Jesus Christ and let Him rule, then we understand what Paul meant when he said that the carnal mind, which resides in the heart, is *'enmity against God.'*

May 18th

Seeing Ourselves as God Sees Us

Romans 2: 1

What we see to condemn in others is either the discernment of the Holy Ghost or the reflection of what we are capable of ourselves. We always notice how obtuse other people are before we notice how obtuse we are ourselves. If we see meanness in others, it is because we are mean ourselves (*see* Romans 2: 1). If we are inclined to be contemptuous over the fraud in others it is because we are frauds ourselves. We have to see ourselves as God sees us. When we do, it keeps us in the right place—"My God, was I ever like that to Thee, so opinionated and conceited, so set on my own ends, and so blind to myself." If these things, which are most unpalatable, are not true, then Calvary is much ado about nothing.

May 19th

Christ Said, "For My Sake"

Matthew 16: 24, 25

Whenever the call is given for abandon to Jesus Christ, people say it is offensive and out of taste. The counterfeit of abandon is that misleading phrase 'Christian service.' I will spend myself for God, I will do anything and everything but the one thing He is asking me to do, viz.: give up my right to myself to Him. We say, "But surely Christian service is a right thing." Immediately we begin to say that, we are off the track. It is the right *Person*, the Lord Jesus Christ, not the right thing. Don't stop short of the Lord Himself— *For My sake*. The great dominating recognition is that my personal self belongs to Jesus. When I receive the Holy Spirit, I receive not merely a possible oneness with Jesus Christ, but a real intense oneness with Him. The point is, will I surrender my individual life entirely to Him? It will mean giving up not only bad things, but things which are right and good (cf. Matt. 19: 29-30). If you have to calculate what you are willing to give up for Jesus Christ, never say you love Him. Jesus Christ asks us to give up the best we have got to Him, our right to ourselves. Self-realization must be renounced in order that Jesus Christ may realize Himself in us.

The Surgery of Providence

Luke 15: 17–20

There is no pain on earth to equal the pain of wounded self-love. Unrequited love is bad enough, but wounded self-love is the cruellest thing to a human being because it shifts the whole foundations of the life. The prodigal son had his self-love wounded; he was full of shame and indignation because he had sunk to such a level. ". . . and I perish with hunger!" There was remorse, but no repentance yet, no thought of his father. "I will arise and go to my father and will say unto him, I have sinned . . . and am no more worthy to be called thy son: . . . And he arose, and came to his father." That is repentance. The surgery of providence had done its work, he was no longer deluded about himself. A repentant soul is never allowed to remain long without being gripped by the love of God.

> 'Man, what is this, and why art thou despairing?
> God shall forgive thee all but thy despair.'

Let the surgery of providence drive you straight to God.

Spiritual Beauty

Luke 2: 40

The presentation of true Christian experience brings us face to face with spiritual beauty; a beauty which can never be forced or imitated, because it is a manifestation from within of a simple relationship to God that is being worked out all the time. There is nothing simple saving a man's relation to God in Christ (2 Cor. 11: 3), and that relationship must never be allowed to be complicated. Our Lord's childhood expresses this spiritual beauty—"And the child grew, and waxed strong, becoming full of wisdom." "And Jesus advanced in wisdom and age" (Luke 2: 40, 52 R.V. marg.). Jesus Christ developed in the way that God intended human beings to develop, and He exhibited the kind of life we ought to live when we have been born from above.

The Knowledge of Good and Evil

Genesis 3: 6

Modern teaching implies that we must be grossly experienced before we can be of any use in the world. That is not true. Jesus Christ understood as no one else has done, but He never ate of the tree of knowledge of good and evil. Our Lord knew good and evil by the life that was in Him; and God intended that man's knowledge of evil should come in the same way as it came to Our Lord, viz.: through the rigorous integrity of obedience to God. It is only when a man is delivered from sin that the Spirit of God begins to give him an understanding of what sin is. When a man is convicted of sin he knows how terrific the havoc is that sin has wrought in him; he knows with what a mighty salvation he has been visited by God; but it is only by obedience to the Holy Spirit that he begins to know what an awful thing sin is.

The Hope of the Otherworldly

Revelation 21: 1-5

The otherworldly person has the belief that everything hoped for or imagined or dreamed about will be absolutely fulfilled and more than fulfilled. This hope runs all through the poetry of the world, it is born of God, but the world does not allow it to be fulfilled in God's way. The saint has not only the vision of the poet, but he submits to God's way of fulfilment, viz.: by the removal of sin, the salvation of sinners, and the sanctification of believers. The danger comes from having barren brains. We have no business to have barren brains. We ought to use our brains until they are thoroughly furnished on God's line. We are tired nowadays of preaching about a future heaven, and have gone to the other extreme and deal only with what we call the practical. We rob ourselves of the tremendous unfathomable certainty that everything God has promised will come to pass. When a Christian has hold of that hope he purifies himself 'even as He is pure.' Nothing can disconcert or upset him because he knows it is only an episode.

Ignorant Innocence
Mark 7: 21–23

Every child born of natural generation is innocent, but it is the innocence of ignorance. Naturally we are in an impaired state, and when our innocence is turned into knowledge we find to our humiliation how tremendously impaired it is. It is the ignorant innocence of determinedly being without the knowledge of God. It is safer to trust God's revelation than our own innocence. Jesus Christ is either the supreme Authority on the human heart, or He is not worth listening to, and He said: "From within out of the heart of man proceed . . ." and then comes that very ugly catalogue. He did not say: "Into the human heart these things are injected," but "from within out of the heart of men, . . . all these evil things proceed." If we trust our innocent ignorance to secure us, it is likely that there will be as life goes on a burst up into our conscious life from underneath which will reveal to us that we are uncommonly like what Jesus Christ says.

True Repentance
Jeremiah 3: 22–25

Repentance means to feel the sorrow which produces new life. Repentance means the miracle of never being again what I was before. It is not sorrow for sin only, but the kind of sorrow that puts an end for ever to the thing over which I sorrow. The only truly repentant man is the holy man. Repentance is spoken of as a gift; it does not spring naturally from the human heart, it is the presence in the human heart of something that springs from the ground of Redemption, and has all the power of a totally new life. Most of us only know remorse, which means I am disgusted with myself; the rarest miracle of God's grace is repentance which by the grace of God turns us into the opposite of what we were.

The Cleansing of the Blood

1 John 1: 7

Cleansing from all sin is far deeper than we can be conscious of: it is cleansing from all sin in the sight of God. The Holy Spirit applies the Atonement to the unconscious realm as well as the conscious, and cleansing from all sin refers to the tremendously profound understanding of sin which only the Holy Ghost has. "If we walk in the light as God is in the light," i.e. with nothing to hide, nothing folded up, then there comes the amazing revelation—"the blood of Jesus Christ His Son *cleanseth us from all sin.*" We are not cleansed more and more from sin; when we are in the light as God is in the light, walking in it, we *are* cleansed from all sin so that God Almighty can see nothing to censure. In our consciousness it works with a keen poignant knowledge of what sin is. The supernatural revelation of Jesus Christ's salvation is that we stand in God's sight free from sin, not in our consciousness; the thing we are conscious of is walking in the light with nothing to hide. As long as we walk there, God sees nothing to censure because the life of His Son is working out in every particular.

May 27th

Progressive Outworking of Holiness

Philippians 2: 12, 13

The great need to-day amongst those of us who profess sanctification is the patience and ability to work out the holiness of God in every detail of the life. When we are first adjusted to God it is on the great big general lines; then the Holy Spirit educates us down to the scruple; He makes us sensitive to things we never thought of before. No matter what our experience may be, we must beware of the curse of being stationary; we have to go on and on in the holy life until we manifest the disposition God has given us in every detail of our lives. The disposition of Jesus enables us to keep all the commandments of God, not some of them.

The Divine Scrutiny

1 Corinthians 4: 5

Are we willing to let God scrutinize us, or are we doing the worst of all things, trying to justify ourselves? People say if they are walking up to the light they have, meaning the light of conscience, they are all right. We may be consciously free from sin, but we are not justified on that account; we may be walking in all the light of conscience, but we are not justified on that account either. We are only justified in the sight of God through the Atonement of Jesus Christ at work in our inner life. God grant we may let His searching scrutiny go through our hearts and spirits until there is nothing that God has not searched. We cannot cabin and confine our lives; there is a purpose in them that is in God's keeping and we know nothing of, but which God will fulfil if we let His tremendous scrutiny go through us and rightly relate us to Himself.

Our Attitude to the Worldly

1 Corinthians 5: 9–13

By Worldly understand the system of men and women in any particular time who order their religion, their business and their social life without any concern as to how it affects Jesus Christ.

We must distinguish between immoral conduct inside and outside the Christian community. We must sternly and unbendingly and unsympathetically rebuke immoral conduct inside the Christian community; outside the Christian community we must bear the shame and humiliation of contact with men vicariously, as Jesus did, that by our lives we may win them to God. Jesus Christ lived amongst the publicans and sinners, people who were guilty of the things Paul condemns (*see* Matt. 11: 19). The condemnation lies in having anything to do with these things inside the Christian community. It is easy to denounce wrong in the world, anyone without a spark of grace can do that, while all the time we may be allowing worldly things in our own lives.

Conviction of Sin in the Saint

Isaiah 6: 5

Conscience is rarely aroused by conviction of sin to begin with; all we can stand until we are saints is conviction of having done wrong things. Sin is much more than an act; sin is a disposition, and only a saint is able to stand conviction of sin. If God gave us conviction of sin, without our having an experience of Redemption, we should be driven insane. The terror of the conviction of sin aroused by the Holy Spirit is that a man knows that God dare not forgive him. It is because we have missed altogether the miracle of the forgiveness of God that we talk so glibly about it—"God is love, therefore of course He will forgive sin." We easily forgive ourselves; we get disgusted for a while and then say—To know all is to forgive all. To know all is to be able to forgive nothing. God cannot forgive unless He does so on a basis that goes deeper than sin, viz.: the basis of Redemption, which means the total alteration of the sinner. If God does not forgive the sinner out of a man, His forgiveness is a farce; and He is not justified in forgiving. The only standard for forgiveness is what it cost God to forgive. It cost Him Calvary. It cost God everything that the Divine nature could give to be able to say, "Thy sins be forgiven thee."

Righteousness That Exceeds

Matthew 5: 20

Our righteousness has to be in excess of the righteousness of the man whose external conduct is blameless according to the law—what does that produce? despair straightaway. When we hear Jesus say "Blessed are the pure in heart," our answer, if we are awake is, "My God, how am I going to be pure in heart? If ever I am to be blameless down to the deepest recesses of my intentions, You must do something mighty in me." That is exactly what Jesus Christ came to do. He did not come to *tell us* to be holy, but to *make* us holy, undeserving of censure in the sight of God. If any man or woman gets there it is by the sheer supernatural grace of God.

The Final Victory

Isaiah 40: 10; Acts 1: 11

The remarkable thing in the record of the Ages that have been, and that are, and that are going to be, is that each Age ends in apparent disaster. The saint alone knows by spiritual intuition that "He doeth all things well," he knows that God reigns, and that the clouds are but the dust of his Father's feet, and he has no need to fear. He feels assured that these catastrophic occurrences are but incidental, and that a higher peace and a purer character are to be the permanent result. He knows that "this same Jesus," who trod this earth with naked feet, "and wrought with human hands the creed of creeds," is coming again, visibly and blessedly coming to earth again, when the petition will be fulfilled, *"Thy kingdom come."* All that men have ever dreamed of Utopias and of Golden Ages will fade into foolish fancies beside the wonder of that blessed Age, that blessed period of Christ's reign among men.

Keep True to the Light

John 12: 35, 36

The discernment of God's call does not come in every moment of life, but only in rare moments; the moments Our Lord spoke of as 'the light' (John 12: 35–6). We have to remain true to what we see in those moments; if we do not we will put back God's purpose in our life. The undercurrent of regret arises when we confer with those who have not heard the call of God, and if we listen to them we get into darkness. The life of Abraham is an illustration of two things: of unreserved surrender to God, and of God's complete possession of a child of His for His own highest ends.

June 3rd

Afraid of Poverty?

Matthew 6: 25-34

To-day we are so afraid of poverty that we never dream of doing anything that might involve us in being poor. We are out of the running of the mediæval monks who took on the vow of poverty. Many of us are poor, but none of us chooses to be. Our attitude is that if we are extravagant a rainy day will come for which we have not laid up. You cannot lay up for a rainy day and justify it in the light of Jesus Christ's teaching. We are not Christians at heart, we don't believe in the wisdom of God, but only in our own. We go in for insurance and economy and speculation, everything that makes us secure in our own wisdom.

June 4th

The Two-edged Sword

Ephesians 6: 17; Hebrews 4: 12

"And take . . . the sword of the Spirit, which is the word of God:" When I have been using "the sword of the Spirit" in a spirit of indignation against another, it is a terrible experience to find the sword suddenly wrested out of my hand and laid about me person-ally by God. Let your personal experience of the work of God's Spirit instruct you at the foot of Calvary; let the light of God riddle you through, then you will never use the word of God to another, never turn the light of God on him, without fear and trembling. "For the word of God is living, and active, and sharper than any two-edged sword, . . ." The word of God is the sword that cuts first in me and then in others. The truth of God can never be escaped from by those who utter it—"Thou therefore that teachest, *teachest thou not thyself?* thou that preachest a man should not steal, *dost thou steal?*"

The Discipline of Human Nature

Ephesians 2: 22; 2 Peter 1: 4-7

We are not delivered from human nature; human nature was created by God, not by the devil; it is impaired, and enfeebled, but it is not sinful. The first creation retains the remnants of God's handiwork; re-creation is the building of a spiritual habitation, "an habitation of God," and all our effort is to be spent in disciplining the natural life in obedience to the new creation wrought in us through the Spirit. If I refuse to make my natural life spiritual by the slow process of obedience, my religious profession becomes a disgusting hypocrisy. Any attempt to build on the natural virtues will ultimately outrage the grace of God, whereas dependence on God means the successful working of God's grace in me. "I do not make void the grace of God," said Paul.

June 6th

The Test of Fruit

Matthew 21: 19; John 15: 8

Leaves of a tree are *a* fruit, but not *the* fruit; they are for the nourishment of the tree itself; that is why in the autumn they push off and sink into the ground where they become disintegrated and are taken into the root again. The fruit proper is never for the tree itself, it is for the husbandman. Woe be to the man who mistakes leaves for fruit! The reason Our Lord cursed the barren fig tree was because it stood as a symbol of leaves being proudly mistaken for fruit (*see* Matthew 21: 19). When we mistake what we do for the fruit, we are deluded; what tells is not what we do, but what is produced by what we do.

The Secret of Reality

John 6: 44-51

There is no delusion in Christian experience, it begins outside me by creating in me an enormous craving, akin to thirst or to hunger. This craving is created by the reality of the Redemption, not by my penetrating insight, but by what Jesus calls 'the drawing of the Father' (John 6: 44). I am brought face to face with Jesus Christ and made to see that God has promised to give the Holy Spirit to them that ask Him. I ask, and I receive by believing the gift of the Holy Spirit, i.e., I receive a complete satisfaction.

No Compromise With Mammon

Matthew 6: 24

"No man can serve two masters;"
"Ye cannot serve God and mammon."

Have we allowed these inexorable decisions of Our Lord to have their powerful way in our thinking? The line of detachment runs all through Our Lord's teaching: You cannot be good and bad at the same time; you cannot serve God and make your own out of the service; you cannot make 'honesty is the best policy' a motive, because immediately you do, you cease to be honest. There is to be only one consideration, a right relationship with God, and see that that relationship is never dimmed. Never compromise with the spirit of mammon. It is easy to associate mammon only with sordid things; mammon is the system of civilized life which organizes itself without any consideration of God (cf. Luke 16: 15).

The School of Calvary

1 Corinthians 2: 2

The call to preach is not because I have a special gift, or because Jesus has sanctified me, but that I have had a glimpse of God's meaning in the Cross, and life can never be the same again. The passion of Paul's preaching is the suffering of God Almighty exhibited in the Cross of Christ. Many who are working for God ought to be learning in the School of Calvary. Paul says—"I determined not to know any thing among you, save Jesus Christ, and Him crucified," —not myself crucified with Christ, that is a mere *et cetera*; the one Figure left is Jesus Christ, and His Cross.

God's Amazing Treatment of His Penitent Child

Luke 15: 20–32

The presentation given in the parable is that the father makes no conditions when the prodigal comes back, neither does he bring home to him any remembrance of the far country—the elder brother does that; it is the revelation of the unfathomable, unalterable, amazing love of God. We would feel much happier in our backslidden condition if we knew that our backsliding had altered God, but we know that immediately we come back we will find Him exactly the same, and that is one of the things that keeps men from coming back. If God would only be angry with us and demand an apology, it would be a gratification to us; when we have done wrong we like to be lashed for it. God never lashes. Jesus does not represent the father as saying, "You have been so wicked that I cannot take you back as my son, I will make you a servant," but as saying, "Bring forth quickly the best robe and put it on him; and put a ring on his hand, and shoes on his feet—and bring the fatted calf, and kill it, and let us eat, and make merry; for this my son was dead, and is alive again; he was lost, and is found."

Discerning God's Point of View
2 Corinthians 4:18

There never was anyone who did not have one moment when all the machinery tumbled away and he saw the meaning of his life. God pays not the remotest attention to our civilized cultures and our attitudes to things, because that is not what we are here for. We are here for one thing—to glorify God. That is where we join issue with the Lord Jesus Christ to-day, and we look at every other thing as life—"What shall we eat? What shall we drink? Wherewithal shall we be clothed?" Our Lord came for one purpose only, to reveal God, and to get men to be spiritually real.

The Divine Estimate of Life
Matthew 25: 1-46

The parable of the ten virgins reveals that it is fatal from our Lord's standpoint to live this life without preparation for the life to come. That is not the exegesis, it is the obvious underlying principle.

The parable of the talents is our Lord's statement with regard to the danger of leaving undone the work of a lifetime.

And the description of the last judgment is the picture of genuine astonishment on the part of both the losers and the gainers of what they had never once thought about.

Strength for the Battle

Ephesians 6: 12; Isaiah 27: 5

We must learn to draw on the supernatural power of God, realizing that our enemies are supernatural, not natural; that our battling is not with difficult circumstances, it is altogether a battling that God is waging for us if we will draw on the supernatural forces. A Christian life lived on any other plane is an impossible life. If we stop drawing, down we go; worry breaks the mind, trouble crushes the spirit, and calamity annihilates the strength of the life, and written over it is God's curse. No Christian has a right to be weak in God's strength.

The Weapon of All Prayer

Ephesians 6: 18

The fundamental basis of the human will deep down is inclined towards God, and prayer works wonders fundamentally. The prayer of the feeblest saint on earth who lives in the Spirit and keeps right with God is a terror to Satan. The very powers of darkness are paralysed by prayer, no spiritualistic seance can succeed in the presence of a humble praying saint. No wonder Satan tries to keep our minds fussy in active work till we cannot think in prayer. It is a vital necessity for Christians to think along the lines on which they pray. The philosophy of prayer is that prayer is *the* work.

The Stronger One

Psalm 2: 4

Satan is overcome not in a battle, but by the easy might of a power greater than his own coming upon him, and that power is none other than our Lord Himself. Every now and again when you look at life from a certain angle it seems as if evil and wrong and legalized iniquity are having it all their own way and you feel that everything must go to pieces; but it doesn't, around it is the sovereignty of God, "Hitherto shalt thou come, but no further." Blessed be the Name of God, evil shall not ultimately triumph! Let evil do its worst, let the arrogance of self-interested iniquity in all shapes and forms surge as it may, but "He that sitteth in the heavens shall laugh: the Lord shall have them in derision." The Spirit of God shatters every power of the world, the flesh and the devil, every power of sin and the domination of Satan.

Divine Concealing and Human Curiosity

Proverbs 25: 2

"It is the glory of God to conceal a thing." God will not have us come with an impatient curiosity. Moral or intellectual or spiritual insanity must result if we push down barriers which God has placed before our spiritual progress is fit for the revelation. This is a day of intolerant inquisitiveness. Men will not wait for the slow, steady, majestic way of the Son of God; they try to enter in by this door and that door. "And one of the elders saith unto me, Weep not: behold, the Lion that is of the tribe of Judah, the Root of David, hath overcome, to open the book and the seven seals thereof" (Rev. 5: 5). The barriers are placed by a Holy God, and He has told us clearly —"Not that way." God grant we may accept His clouds and mysteries, and be led into His inner secrets by obedient trust.

Misjudging God's Ways

Psalm 97: 11, 12

If we go on obeying God, we shall find that 'light is sown for the righteous.' We are so impatient—"I thought God's purpose was to make me full of happiness and joy." It is, but it is happiness and joy from God's standpoint, not from ours. God always ignores the present perfection for the ultimate perfection. We bring God to the bar of our judgment and say hard things about Him—"Why does God bring thunderclouds and disasters when we want green pastures and still waters?" Bit by bit we find, behind the clouds, the Father's feet; behind the lightning, an abiding day that has no night; behind the thunder a still small voice that comforts with a comfort that is unspeakable.

Treasures of Darkness

Isaiah 45: 3

It is the glory of God to conceal His treasures in embarrassments, i.e., in things that involve us in difficulty. "I will give thee the treasures of darkness." We would never have suspected that treasures were hidden there, and in order to get them we have to go through things that involve us in perplexity. There is nothing more wearying to the eye than perpetual sunshine, and the same is true spiritually. The valley of the shadow gives us time to reflect, and we learn to praise God for the valley because in it our soul was restored in its communion with God. God gives us a new revelation of His kindness in the valley of the shadow. What are the days and the experiences that have furthered us most? The days of green pastures, of absolute ease? No, they have their value; but the days that have furthered us most in character are the days of stress and cloud.

The Only Answer

John 1: 29

Where are we in regard to the personal experience of the baptism of the Holy Ghost? If Jesus Christ had said to us, "All you need to do is to be as holy as you can, overcome sin as far as you can, and I will overlook the rest," no intelligent man under heaven would accept such a salvation. But He says—"Be ye perfect"; "Love your enemies"; "Be so pure that lust is an impossibility." Instantly every heart calls back, "My God, who is sufficient for these things?" Oceans of penitential tears, mountains of good works, all powers and energy sink down till they are under the feet of the Lord Jesus, and, incarnate in John the Baptist, they all point to Him—"Behold the Lamb of God, which taketh away the sins of the world."

Complete Deliverance Possible

2 Corinthians 9: 8-11

If Jesus Christ cannot deliver from sin, if He cannot adjust us perfectly to God as He says He can; if He cannot fill us with the Holy Ghost until there is nothing that can ever appeal again in sin or the world or the flesh, then He has misled us. But blessed be the Name of God, He can! He can so purify, so indwell, so merge with Himself, that only the things that appeal to Him appeal to you. To all other appeals there is the sentence of death, you have nothing to answer. When you come amongst those whose morality and uprightness crown them the lord of their own lives, there is no affinity with you, and they leave you alone.

The Rest of Patience and Faith

Isaiah 30: 15

To wait upon God is the perfection of activity. We are told to "rest in the Lord," not to rust. We talk of resting in the Lord but it is often only a pious expression; in the Bible, resting in the Lord is the patience of godly confidence. "In returning and rest shall ye be saved; . . . But ye said, No, for we will flee upon horses;" i.e., we will take the initiative. When we take the initiative we put our wits on the throne, we do not worship God.

"Wait Only Upon God"

Psalm 62: 5

Is silent prayer to us an experience of waiting upon God, or is it a 'cotton wool' experience, utterly dim and dark? A time which we simply endure until it is over? If you want discerning vision about anything, you have to make an effort and call in your wandering attention. Mental wool-gathering can be stopped immediately the will is roused. Prayer is an effort of will, and the great battle in prayer is the over-coming of mental wool-gathering. We put things down to the devil when we should put them down to our own inability to concentrate. "My soul, wait thou only upon God," i.e., "pull yourself together and be silent unto God."

Through the Cross to . . . ?

Philippians 3: 7–10

How much more is there to know, after sanctification? Everything! Before sanctification we know nothing, we are simply put in the place of knowing; that is, we are led *up* to the Cross; in sanctification we are led *through* the Cross—for what purpose? For a life of outpouring service to God. The characteristic of a saint after identification with the death of Jesus is that he is brought down from the ineffable glory of the heavenly places into the valley to be crushed and broken in service for God. We are here with no right to ourselves, for no spiritual blessing for ourselves; we are here for one purpose only—to be made servants of God as Jesus was. Have we as saints allowed our minds to be brought face to face with this great truth?

The Miracle of Restoration

Joel 2: 25

Many a sensitive soul has been driven into insanity through anguish of mind because he has never realized what Jesus Christ came to do, and all the asylums in the world will never touch them in the way of healing; the only thing that will is the realization of what the death of Jesus means, viz., that the damage we have done may be repaired through the efficacy of His Cross. Jesus Christ has atoned for all, and He can make it good in us, not only as a gift but by a participation on our part. The miracle of the grace of God is that He can make the past as though it had never been; He can "restore the years that the locust hath eaten, the cankerworm, and the caterpiller, and the palmerworm."

June 25th

The Mystery of His Desolation

Mark 15: 34; Hebrews 2: 9

The cry on the Cross, "My God, My God, why hast Thou forsaken Me?" is unfathomable to us. The only ones—and I want to say this very deliberately—the only ones who come near the threshold of understanding the cry of Jesus are not the martyrs, they knew that God had not forsaken them, His presence was so wonderful; not the lonely missionaries who are killed or forsaken, they experience exultant joy, for God is with them when men forsake them: the only ones who come near the threshold of understanding the experience of Godforsakenness are men like Cain—"My punishment is greater than I can bear;" men like Esau, ". . . an exceeding bitter cry;" men like Judas. Jesus Christ knew and tasted to a fuller depth than any man could ever taste what it is to be separated from God by sin.

June 26th

Our Magnanimous God

Matthew 5: 45

In the first place, our great God's blessings fall, like His rain, on evil and good alike. The great blessings of health, genius, prosperity, all come from His overflowing grace, and not from the condition of the character of the recipients. For instance, if health were a sign that a man is right with God, we should lose all distinction as to what a good character is, for many bad men enjoy good health. It is humbling and illuminating to catch the profound meaning of the Apostle Paul's statement to Timothy: "If we believe not, yet He abideth faithful: He cannot deny Himself" (2 Timothy 2: 13). All man's unfaithfulness, all man's sins,

> . . . alters God no more
> Than our dimmed eyes can quench the stars in heaven

There is no element of the vindictive in our great and good God.

Blessings That Lead to Repentance

Romans 2: 4

One of the great marks that the blessings of God are being rightly used is that they lead us to repentance. ". . . not knowing that the goodness of God leadeth thee to repentance?" Repentance in the New Testament sense means just the difference between a sanctified and an unsanctified soul. The only repentant man in the New Testament sense is the holy man, one who is rightly related to God by the Atonement of Jesus and has become a written epistle, 'known and read of all men.' How many of us have allowed the goodness of God to lead us to repentance? Or are we so enjoying the blessings of God, like the beasts of the field, taking them as our due and not seeing behind them the great loving hand of God, Whose heart is overflowing in tremendous love?

Glorious Uncertainty, But Sure of God

2 Timothy 1: 12

In the realm of belief, whenever I become certain of my creeds, I kill the life of God in my soul, because I cease to believe in God and believe in my belief instead. All through the Bible the realm of the uncertain is the realm of joy and delight; the certainty of belief brings distress. Certainty of God means uncertainty in life; while certainty in belief makes us uncertain of God. Certainty is the mark of the common-sense life; gracious uncertainty is the mark of the spiritual life, and they must both go together. Mathematics is the rule of reason and common sense, but faith and hope is the rule of the spiritual. "It is not yet made manifest what we shall be"—we are gloriously uncertain of the next step, but we are certain of God. Immediately we abandon to God and do the duty that lies nearest, He packs our lives with surprises all the time.

June 29th

The Blood of Christ, the Blood of God

Acts 20: 28

It was not the blood of a martyr, not the blood of goats and calves, that was shed, but 'the blood of Christ.' The very life of God was shed for the world—"the church of God which He purchased with His own blood" (Acts 20: 28). All the perfections of the essential nature of God were in that blood; all the holiest attainments of man were in that blood. The death of Jesus reaches away down underneath the deepest sin human nature ever committed. This aspect of the death of Jesus takes us into a spiritual domain beyond the threshold of the thinking of the majority of us.

June 30th

No Answer: But Vision

Job 42: 5, 6

"Now mine eyes seeth Thee, and I abhor my words," i.e. "I abhor the things I was certain of, I abhor myself for being so obstinately certain that I knew; but now I see." In looking at Job's circumstances the curious thing is, he asks conundrum after conundrum, and instead of their being solved, the providence of God hurls more problems at him, till at last Job says, "Now I see." He did not perceive anything in the logical line, he simply found that the interpretation lay with God. Job discerned that truth is never gained by intellect, but by moral conscientiousness. Truth is always a vision that arises in the basis of the moral nature, never in the intellect. Immediately we are rightly related to God in moral relationships, instantly we perceive.

The Secret of True Unity

1 Corinthians 12: 13

"For by one Spirit are we all baptized into one body." The baptism with the Holy Ghost is not only a personal experience, it is an experience which makes individual Christians one in the Lord. The only way saints can meet together as one is through the baptism of the Holy Ghost, not through external organizations. The end of all divisions in work for God is when He changes fever into white-heated fervour. Oh, the foolish fever there is these days! Organizing this, organizing that; a fever of intense activity for God. What is wanted is the baptism with the Holy Ghost which will mean Our Lord's prayer in John 17 is answered—"that they all may be one; as Thou, Father, are in Me, and I in Thee, that they also may be one in us" (v. 21).

Submission to Human Institutions

1 Peter 2: 13, 14

Peter's statements in these verses are remarkable, and they are statements the modern Christian does not like. He is outlining what is to be the conduct of saints in relation to the moral institutions based on the government of man by man. No matter, he says, what may be the condition of the community to which you belong, behave yourself as a saint in it. Many people are righteous as individuals, but they ignore the need to be righteous in connection with human institutions. Paul continually dealt with insubordination in spiritual people. Degeneration in the Christian life comes in because of this refusal to recognize the insistence God places on obedience to human institutions. Take the institution of home life. Home is God's institution, and He says, "Honour thy father and thy mother." Are we fulfilling our duty to our parents as laid down in God's Book?

After Experience, Knowledge

1 Corinthians 6: 19

I have to see that I instruct myself regarding these revelations which are only interpreted to me by the Holy Ghost, never by my natural wisdom. There are some saints who are ideally actual, i.e., instructed as well as sanctified, and living in unsullied communion with God, and there are others who are like Ephraim, "a cake not turned." Once let it dawn on your mind that your body is the temple of the Holy Ghost and instantly the impossible becomes possible; the things you used to pray about, you no longer pray about, but *do*. As in the natural world, so in the spiritual, knowledge is power. All we need to *experience* is that we have 'passed out of death into life': what we need to *know* takes all Time and Eternity. "And this is life eternal, that they might know Thee the only true God. . . ." (John 17: 3). Begin to know Him now.

True Freedom, Not Independence

1 Corinthians 6: 12

We call liberty allowing the other fellow to please himself to the same extent as we please ourselves. True liberty is the ability earned by practice to do the right thing. There is no such thing as a gift of freedom; freedom must be earned. The counterfeit of freedom is independence. When the Spirit of God deals with sin, it is independence that He touches, that is why the preaching of the Gospel awakens resentment as well as craving. Independence must be blasted right out of a Christian, there must be only liberty, which is a very different thing. Spiritually, liberty means the ability to fulfil the law of God, and it establishes the rights of other people.

All Things Together for Good

Romans 8: 28

The marvellous thing about the life of God in us is that there is no reaction of exhaustion, it is a continual pouring in all the time. If we work from our own source of energy in a very short time we become artificial, played out, but if we work from the real source of energy, everything that transpires produces 'smeddum,' a good old Scotch word meaning grit, courage, pluck. Some of us say "I have tried to do all I can for my Church, or my Sunday School class, but it has all failed and I'm going to give it up." That is enervation, i.e., vitality ebbing away because of stagnation somewhere in the vital organs. As long as we whine at circumstances we shall experience the extraordinary trick of providence which keeps us in those circumstances until we learn our lesson. If your circumstances are dark blue just now, remember the time when they were bright pink. It is not the dark blue circumstances that work for our good or the bright pink ones, it is the 'togetherness' that does it.

Intercessory Introspection

Psalm 139: 23, 24

It is a marvellous moment in a man's life when he knows he is explored by God. The tendency in us which makes us want to examine ourselves and know the springs of our thoughts and motives takes the form of prayer, "Search me, O God." The Psalmist speaks of God as the Creator Who knows the vast universe outside, and of His omnipresence, but he does not end there, he asks this great God to explore him. There is something infinitely more mysterious to the Psalmist than the great universe outside, and that is the mystery of his own heart. There are mountain peaks in my soul, he implies, that I cannot climb; there are ocean depths I cannot fathom; there are possibilities in my heart that terrify me; therefore, O God, search me out. That is intercessory introspection.

His Yoke Beneath the Cross
Matthew 11: 28, 29

The only place we shall find rest is in the direct education by Jesus in His Cross. A new delight springs up in any saint who suffers the yoke of Christ. Beware of dissipating that yoke and making it mean the yoke of a martyr. It is the yoke of a person who owes all he has to the Cross of Christ. Paul wore the yoke when he said, "For I determined not to know anything among you, save Jesus Christ, and Him crucified." "Take My yoke upon you"—it is the one yoke men will not wear.

Have I taken the yoke of Christ upon me, and am I walking in the innocent light that comes only from the Spirit of God through the Atonement?

Spiritual Gluttony
Isaiah 33: 16; Amos 8: 11

Two things the Bible states are sure for men if they obey God—bread and water (see Isaiah 33: 16); that is all God has promised us. Look over the history of civilizations and you will find every disaster has come by taking more. A spiritual application may be made along this line—'a famine of hearing the words of the Lord' strikes every soul that has departed from the living God and dwelt by pleasant spiritual experiences—God's word dead to you, no inspiration about it; prayer dead, spiritual communion dead, you wait and long and pray and nothing happens, everything languishing and dying. You will find if sin has not been the cause, there has been a selfish glutting of your soul on experiences instead of going on to know God Who gave you the experiences. We refuse to eat the old corn of the land, we prefer manna—that God should always do some exceptional thing for us.

An Eternal Principle

Matthew 16: 25

We must bear in mind that Our Lord in His teaching reveals unalterable and eternal principles. In Matthew 16: 25—"For whosoever would save his life shall lose it: and whosoever shall lose his life for My sake shall find it"—Jesus says that the eternal principle of human life is that something must be sacrificed; if we won't sacrifice the natural life, we do the spiritual. Our Lord is not speaking of a punishment to be meted out, He is revealing what is God's eternal principle at the back of human life. We may rage and fret, as men have done, against God's just principles, or we may submit and accept and go on; but Jesus reveals that these principles are as unalterable as God Himself.

My Attitude to Another's Sin

Jeremiah 14: 7; 1 John 5: 16

"We have sinned against Thee." There is a difference between a moralist's and a Christian's condemnation of sin. A spiritual Christian always feels the unmitigated horror of the sin of another. A moralist never does, to him it is an occasion to 'lambast' something that is wrong. A Christian knows that the possibilities of every sin ever committed are in him but for the grace of God. The condemnation of sin before we are saved is bitter, intense, and proud. After we are saved, the sins of others come upon us with the twofold weight of the possibility of doing the like ourselves, and the possibility of vicarious intercession.

"Why shouldest Thou be . . . as a mighty man that cannot save?" (v. 9). Why does not God speak? This is not atheism, but the agony of a human heart getting into the secret of the Cross.

July 11th

Watching and Waiting

Habbakuk 2: 1

Watch for God's answers to your prayers, and not only watch but wait. When God calls upon you to pray, when He gives you the vision, when He gives you an understanding of what He is going to do through you in your Sunday-school class, in your Church or home—watch. How many of us have had to learn by God's reproof, by God's chastisement, the blunder of conferring with flesh and blood. Are you discouraged where you are, worker? Then get upon this tower with God, and watch, and wait. The meaning of waiting in both Old and New Testament is 'standing under,' actively enduring. It is not standing with folded arms doing nothing; it is not saying, "In God's good time it will come to pass"—that often means, "In my abominably lazy time I let God work." Waiting means standing under, in active strength, enduring till the answer comes.

July 12th

Our Loyalty to His Royalty

John 18: 37 (R.V. marg.)

Jesus Christ is not only Saviour, He is King, and He has the right to exact anything and everything from us at His own discretion. We talk about the joys and comforts of salvation; Jesus Christ talks about taking up the cross and following Him. Whenever Our Lord talks about discipleship He prefaces it with an 'If'—'you need not unless you like.' It is always easier in certain crises to be 'Demas' than a devoted disciple. Very few of us know anything about loyalty to Jesus Christ. "For My sake"—that is what makes the iron saint. We look upon Jesus Christ as the best Example of the Christian life; we do not conceive of Him as Almighty God Incarnate, with all power in heaven and on earth. We deal with Him as if He were one of ourselves; we do not take off the shoes from our feet when He speaks. Jesus Christ is Saviour, and He saves us into His own absolute and holy lordship.

The Motive Behind Our Righteousness

1 John 3: 7

". . . he that *doeth* righteousness is righteous." There are different kinds of intention, e.g., outer and inner; immediate and remote; direct and indirect. The righteous man is the one whose inner intention is clearly revealed in his outer intention, there is no duplicity, no internal hypocrisy. A man's outer intention is easily discernible by other people; his inner intention needs to be continually examined. The marvel of the grace of God is that it can alter the mainspring of our make-up; then when that is altered we must foster in ourselves those intentions which spring from the Spirit of Jesus and make our nervous system carry them out. The Holy Spirit will bring us to the practical test, it is not that I *say* I am righteous, but that I prove I am in my deeds.

Bondslaves of Jesus

Philippians 1: 13

The passion of Christianity is that I deliberately sign away my own rights and become a bondslave of Jesus Christ. Any fool can insist on his rights, and any devil will see that he gets them; but the Sermon on the Mount means that the only right the saint will insist on is the right to give up his rights. That is the New Testament idea of sanctification, and that is why so few get anywhere near the baptism with the Holy Ghost. "I want to be baptized with the Holy Ghost so that I may be of use"—then it is all up.

Mastered by the Master

John 13: 13-17

Whenever a man is mastered by Jesus Christ you have a man "with breast and back as either should be," no whimperer, no sentimentalist, no pietist, but a man of God. That can only be produced by the mastership of Jesus Christ. The curious thing about Our Lord is that He never insists on our obedience. When we begin to usurp authority and say, 'You must' and 'you shall' it is a sure sign that we are out of touch with the supreme Authority. If you are in a position of authority and people are not obeying you, the greatest heart-searching you can have is the realization that the blame does not lie with them, but with you; there is a leakage going on spiritually. Get right with God yourself, and every other one will get in touch with God through you.

Self Truly Realized in Love to God

Mark 12: 30, 31

Man was created to be the friend and lover of God and for no other end, and until he realizes this he will go through turmoil and upset. Human nature must rise to its own Source, the bosom of God, and Jesus Christ by His Redemption brings it back there. God is the only One who has the right to myself and when I love Him with all my heart and soul and mind and strength, self in its essence is realized. All the teaching of Jesus is woven around self; I have a moral self-love to preserve for God. Not, 'Oh, I'm of no account,' 'a worm,' that would spell self-less-ness. "I hold not my life of any account, as dear unto myself," says Paul, "so that I may accomplish my course, and the ministry which I received from the Lord Jesus, to testify the gospel of the grace of God." That is, he refused to use himself for any other interest but God's, and for that which glorified God.

What Is Perfect Love?

1 John 4: 8–12

But let the lowliest soul whose influence apparently amounts to nothing get rightly related to God, and out of him will flow rivers of living water which he does not see, but one day we shall find that it is those lives which have been spreading the lasting benediction. *"Love is of God"*; it never came from the devil and never can go to the devil. When I am rightly related to God, the more I love the more blessing does He pour out on other lives. The reward of love is the capacity to pour out more love all the time, 'hoping for nothing again.' That is the essential nature of perfect love.

The true import of love is the surrender of my self, I go out of myself in order to live in and for God. To be indwelt by the Spirit of Jesus means I am willing to quit my own abode from the self-interested standpoint and live only in and for God.

Self Sacrifice or Obedience

1 Samuel 15: 22; Hebrews 10: 5–7

"Behold, to obey is better than sacrifice." Self-sacrifice may be simply a disease of the nerves, a morbid self-consciousness which is the obverse of intense selfishness. Our Lord never confounds selfishness and self. Whenever I make self-sacrifice the aim and end of my life, I become a traitor to Jesus; instead of placing Him as my Lodestar I place Him as an example, One who helps me to sacrifice myself. I am not saved to sacrifice; I am saved to fulfil my destiny in Christ. It is much easier to sacrifice myself, to efface myself, than to do God's will in His way.

Perfectly Fit, But . . .

Philippians 3: 15

"Let us therefore as many as be perfect . . ."—Paul implies, "Now remember though you have been perfectly adjusted to God through the Redemption, you have attained to nothing yet." The idea is that of a marathon runner, practising and practising until he is perfectly fit; when he is perfectly fit, he hasn't begun his race, he is only perfectly fit to begin. By regeneration we are put into perfect relation with God, then it is the same human nature, working on the same lines, but with a different mainspring. "Not that I have already obtained, or am already made perfect:" that is the perfection of consummation, "I haven't got there yet," says Paul; "but I press on if so be that I may apprehend that for which also I was apprehended by Christ Jesus."

False Shepherds and True

Ezekiel 34: 2–8; John 21: 16

"Should not the shepherds feed the sheep?" (ch. 34: 2). In the New Testament the terms 'shepherd' and 'sheep' are applied not to kings and nations, but to the disciples of Jesus. When Our Lord commissioned Peter He did not tell him to go and save souls, but—"Feed My sheep; tend My lambs; guard My flock." We have to be careful lest we rebel against the commission to disciple men to Jesus and become energetic proselytizers to our own way of thinking—"but the shepherds fed themselves, and fed not My sheep;" (v. 8). When we stand before God will He say, "Well done, good and faithful servant"? or will He say, "You have not been a shepherd of My sheep, you have fed them for your own interest, exploited them for your own creed"? When a soul gets within sight of Jesus Christ, leave him alone.

Fulfilling the Law Through Christ

Philippians 3: 9

Saul of Tarsus did easily what other Pharisees did, but his conscience would not allow him to be a hypocrite easily. His ardent nature tried to make his inner life come up to the standard of the law, and the tragedy of his failure is expressed in Romans 7. No one was ever so introspective, so painfully conscious of his weakness and inability to keep the law, consequently when he says "Christ is the end of the law unto righteousness," he is making the most intensely practical statement that could be made. He is stating the fact that Christ had planted in him as a sheer gift of God's grace the life which enabled him now easily to fulfill all the law of God—"not having a righteousness of mine own, . . . but that which is through faith in Christ." *'Imputed'* with Paul always means *'imparted.'*

The Subtle Sin of Pride

Ezekiel 28: 2

Pride in its most estimable as well as its most debased form is self-deification; it is not a yielding to temptation from without, but a distinct alteration of relationships within. Watch where you are not willing to give up your self-confident obstinacy in little things, and you will know how much pride there is in your heart, how much you will set your moral teeth against God's providential order—"I won't yield"; "I won't for a second allow anyone to usurp my rights." To that life will come the revelation of God as an enemy. If we have had detected in us any lurking of pride, when are we going to break from it? We will have to break some day, why not now?

Are We Going on to Apprehend?

Philippians 3: 12

Paul reverted to one thing only—"When it was the good pleasure of God, . . . to reveal His Son in me," then he never bothered about himself any more. We try to lose ourselves and efface ourselves by an effort; Paul did not efface himself by an effort, his interest in himself simply died right out when he became identified with Christ and Him crucified. We are all more or less keenly interested in the work of grace in our souls, but the reason we don't go on to 'apprehend that for which we were apprehended by Christ' is that there are whole tracts of our nature which have never been fused by the fire of God into one central purpose. How long it takes till all our powers are at one depends on one thing only, viz., obedience.

The Strangeness of His 'Faithfulness'

Luke 18: 1-8

Human life is not made up of right and wrong, but of things which are not quite clear—"I do not know what God would have me do in this matter." Stand off in faith that what Jesus said is true —*everyone that asks receives*, and in the meantime do the duty that lies nearest, waiting and watching. If the friendship of God is shrouded and it looks as if He is not going to do anything, then remain dumb. The real problems are very heavy. Instead of God being a Father loving and kind, it looks at times as if He were totally indifferent. Remember, God has bigger issues at stake on the ground of His Redemption than the particular setting in which we ask. In the meantime we do not know what God is doing, but we are certain that what Jesus says is true. "If ye then, being evil, know how to give good gifts unto your children, how much more shall your Heavenly Father give the Holy Spirit to them that ask Him?" When we are the possessors of the Holy Spirit, we shall justify God all through.

July 25th

Blessing Through the Word
Isaiah 55: 10, 11

". . . giveth seed to the sower." God's word is as a seed. The 'seed-thought' idea is one that preachers and evangelists need to remember. We imagine we have to plough the field, sow the seed, reap the grain, bind it into sheaves, put it through the threshing machine, make the bread—all in one discourse. "For herein is the saying true, One soweth, and another reapeth" said our Lord. Let each one be true to the calling given him by God. The truth is we don't believe God can do His work without us. We are so anxious about the word, so anxious about the people who have accepted the word; we need not be, if we have preached what is a word of God it is not our business to apply it, the Holy Spirit will apply it.

July 26th

The Living Word in the Written Word
2 Peter 1: 20

Just as Jesus Christ is the final revelation of God, so the Bible is the final revelation interpreting Him. Our Lord Jesus Christ (The Word of God) and the Bible (the accompanying revelation) stand or fall together, they can never be separated without fatal results. The words of the Bible apart from being interpreted by the Word of God, are worse than lifeless, they kill (2 Corinthians 3: 6). But when a soul is born from above and lifted to the atmosphere of the domain where our Lord lives, the Bible becomes its native air, its words become the storehouse of omnipotence, its commands and prophecies become alive, its limitless horizons brace the heart and mind to a new consciousness, its comforts in Psalms and prayers and exhortations delight the whole man. And better than all, the Lord Jesus Christ becomes the altogether Lovely One, it is in His light that we see light, it is in Him that we become new creatures. He who is the Word of God unfolds to us the revelation of God until we say in sacred rapture, "I hold in my hands the Thought of God."

The Shadow of His Fatherhood

Luke 11: 11, 12

Jesus says there are times when our Heavenly Father will appear as if He were a most unnatural father, callous and indifferent—I asked for bread and He gave me a stone, and there is a shadow on His Fatherhood. But remember, says Jesus, I have told you— *everyone that asks receives.* When we get into spiritual confusion the usual way out is to say we have made a blunder, and we go back instead of forward. "I don't know what to do; I am up against a stone wall." Will you 'hang in' to what Jesus said? If there is a shadow on the face of the Fatherhood of God just now, remain confident that ultimately He will give His clear issue as Jesus said. It is not a question of black or white, of right or wrong; of being in communion or out of communion; but a question of God taking us by a way which in the meantime we do not understand.

Faith and Prayer in the Details

Isaiah 37: 14; 1 Peter 1: 7

Faith is the trend of the life all through, and everything that is not 'hid with Christ in God' is against it. The trial of faith always comes in such a way that it is a perplexity to know what to do. You get advice that sounds wise, it has your welfare in view, everything seems right, and yet there is the feeling that there is an error at the heart of it.

"And Hezekiah received the letter from the hand of the messengers, and read it: and Hezekiah went up unto the house of the Lord, and spread it before the Lord" (v. 14). If any letter is not important enough to be 'spread before the Lord' it is too small to annoy you. If I have not prayed about things so ridiculously small that I almost blush to mention them, I have not learned the first lesson in prayer.

July 29th

Our Anguish in God's Fire

Job 7: 12–18

Job gives utterance to a mood which is not foreign to us when he says, "Am I a sea, or a whale, that Thou settest a watch over me?" In certain moods of anguish the human heart says to God, "I wish You would let me alone, why should I be used for things which have no appeal to me?" In the Christian life we are not being used for our own designs at all, but for the fulfilment of the prayer of Jesus Christ. He has prayed that we might be 'one with Him as He is one with the Father,' consequently God is concerned only about that one thing, and He never says 'By your leave.' Whether we like it or not, God will burn us in His fire until we are as pure as He is, and it is during the process that we cry, as Job did, "I wish You would leave me alone." God is the only Being who can afford to be misunderstood; we cannot, Job could not, but God can.

July 30th

The Supplanter Becomes a Warrior

Genesis 32: 27

The confession has to be made—"That is my name—sneak, supplanter;" there is no palliation. This is full and profound and agonizing repentance. Jacob had to get to the place where he willingly confesses before God the whole guilt of his usurping the birthright. "And he said, Thy name shall be called no more Jacob, but Israel: for thou hast striven with God and with men, and hast prevailed." The warrior of God is not the man of muscle and a strong jaw, but the man of unutterable weakness, the man who knows he has not any power, he instantly becomes a warrior of God. Jacob is no longer strong in himself, he is strong only in the Lord; his life is no longer marked by his own striving but by reliance on God. You cannot imitate reliance on God.

The Renewal of the Mind

Romans 12: 2

Always remember that Jesus Christ's statements force an issue of will and conscience first, and only as we obey is there the understanding with the mind (*see* John 7: 17). The challenge to the will comes in the matter of study, as long as you remain in the 'stodge' state there is no mental progress—"I am overwhelmed by the tremendous amount there is to know and it's no use my going on." If you will forge through that stage you will suddenly turn a corner where everything that was difficult and perplexing becomes as clear as a lightning flash, but it all depends on whether you will forge ahead. When people say, "Preach us the simple Gospel," what they mean is, "Preach us the thing we have always heard, the thing that keeps us sound asleep, we don't want to see things differently"; then the sooner the Spirit of God sends a thrust through their stagnant minds the better. Continual renewal of mind is the only healthy state for a Christian. Beware of the ban of finality about your present views.

The Only Safe Place

Isaiah 14: 32

"The Lord hath founded Zion, and in her shall the afflicted of His people take refuge" (ch. 14: 32). Just as Zion is spoken of as the central place of safety for the nations, so the only safe place for the saint, and it is as safe as God Himself, is the secret place of the Most High, abiding under the shadow of the Almighty (cf. Psalm 125: 1-2). The same great majestic note is brought out in Psalm 46— "Therefore will not we fear, though . . ." It is the grand position got from the great God.

Undisturbed in Disturbance

Isaiah 25: 4, 5

The great thing about faith in God is that it keeps a man undisturbed in the midst of disturbance. Every now and again God lets loose the hounds of hell all around you, and if you are His child, indwelt by His Spirit, you will experience the truth that Isaiah proclaims, viz., that all the forces outside you are futile because they are less powerful than the indwelling of God (*see* 1 John 4: 4). No matter what may be the changing of forceful interests all around, the work of God's grace stands true in His servants.

The Only Thing That Remains

Luke 12: 20

We estimate by what a man possesses; God's only concern is what a man *is*. There is only one thing that will endure and that is personality, no possessions, no pretence, nothing in the way of what men call greatness will last. All the rest is trappings, in their right place, great and good trappings, but Satan wants to keep our minds on them. Holiness in character is the only thing that will remain. Some of us will have a spiritual character so microscopic that it will take the archangels to find it!

August 4th

Carefully Careless

Matthew 6: 25-34

The most seriously minded Christian is the one who has just become a Christian; the mature saint is just like a young child, absolutely simple and joyful and gay. Read the Sermon on the Mount —"Take no thought," (i.e. no care) "for your life." The word 'care' has within it the idea of something that buffets. The Christianity of Jesus Christ refuses to be careworn. Our Lord is indicating that we have to be carefully careless about everything saving our relationship to Him.

August 5th

The Road Back to Yesterday

Joel 2: 25

Forgiveness does not mean merely that I am saved from sin and made right for heaven; forgiveness means that I am forgiven into a recreated relationship to God.

Do I believe that God can deal with my 'yesterday,' and make it as though it had never been? I either do not believe He can, or I do not want Him to. Forgiveness, which is so easy for us to accept, cost God the agony of Calvary. When Jesus Christ says "Sin no more," He conveys the power that enables a man not to sin any more, and that power comes by right of what He did on the Cross.

The 'Profane Man'

Hebrews 12: 16

"I loved Jacob"—God loves the man who needs Him. Esau was satisfied with what he was; Jacob wanted more than he was. Esau never saw visions, or wrestled with angels, although God was as near to him as He was to Jacob. He refused to sacrifice anything to the spiritual. Esau could never think of anything but the present; he was willing to sell the promise of the future for a mess of pottage, and thereby he wronged himself more than Jacob did.

The Wonder of Bethel

Genesis 28: 16, 17

'This place' means just where it is not within the bounds of imagination to infer that God would be. "And he called the name of that place Beth-el . . ." (v. 19) "because there God was revealed unto him" (ch. 35: 7). "Every house of God is a gate of heaven where the impossible and the miraculous become the natural breath." There is always an amazed surprise when we find what God brings with Him when He comes, He brings everything! (cf. John 14: 23).

Receiving His Peace

John 14: 27

The disciples, like many to-day, were not in a state to provide their own inner peace. There are times when inner peace is based on ignorance; but when we awake to the troubles of life, which more than ever before surge and heave in threatening billows, inner peace is impossible unless it is received from our Lord. When our Lord spoke peace, He made peace. His words are ever 'spirit and life.' Have you ever received what He spoke?

The God of Jacob

Psalm 46: 11

When we come to consider it, the phrase 'the God of Jacob' is the greatest possible inspiration; it has in it the whole meaning of the Gospel of Jesus Christ, who said He came not to call the righteous but sinners. Had we been left with such phrases as 'the God of Joseph,' or 'the God of Daniel,' it would have spelt hopeless despair for most of us; but 'the God of Jacob' means—'God is *my* God,' the God of the sneak, not only of the noble characters. From the sneak to entire sanctification is the miracle of the grace of God.

Telling God What He Knows

Isaiah 37: 14-20

To the rationalist it is ridiculous to pray to God about everything; behind the ridicule is the devil to keep us from knowing the road when the crisis comes. Hezekiah knew the road. In his prayer (vv. 16-20) Hezekiah tells God what he knows God knows already. That is the meaning of prayer—I tell God what I know He knows in order that I may get to know it as He does (cf. Matthew 6: 8). It is not true to say that a man learns to pray in calamities, he never does; he calls on God to deliver him, but he does not pray (*see* Psalm 107: 6, 13, 19); a man only learns to pray when there is no calamity.

Man's Destiny: Salvation or Damnation?

Genesis 31: 3

"And the Lord said unto Jacob, Return."

No man's destiny is made for him, each man makes his own. Fatalism is the deification of moral cowardice which arises from a refusal to accept the responsibility for choosing either of the two destined ends for the human race—salvation or damnation. The power of individual choice is the secret of human responsibility. I can choose which line I will go on, but I have no power to alter the destination of that line when once I have taken it—yet I always have the power to get off one line on to the other.

The Sense of the Irreparable

Job 3: 2, 3

It is a sad thing that Job is facing, and it seems that the only reasonable thing he can do is to mourn the day of his birth. With some people suffering is imaginary, but with Job it has actually happened, and his curse is the real deep conviction of his spirit—"Would to God I had never been born!" The sense of the irreparable is one of the greatest agonies in human life. Adam and Eve entered into the sense of the irreparable when the gates of Paradise clanged behind them. Cain cried out—"My punishment is greater than I can bear." Esau "found no place of repentance, though he sought it diligently with tears." There are things in life which are irreparable; there is no road back to yesterday.

Strangers and Sojourners

Genesis 23: 4; Hebrews 11: 13

The phrase Abraham uses, 'a stranger and sojourner,' is the inner meaning of the term 'Hebrew.' Abraham could never say that he was at home in Canaan, he left his home never to find another on earth. The thought of pilgrimage sank deep into the Hebrew mind, and the note of the sojourner is essentially the note of the Christian. Instead of being pilgrims and strangers on the earth, we become citizens of this order of things and entrench ourselves there, and the statements of Jesus have no meaning. The genius of the Spirit of God is to make us pilgrims.

In dealing with the life of Abraham neither faith nor common sense must be our guide, but God Who unites both in the alchemy of personal experience. To be guided by common sense alone is fanatical; both common sense and faith have to be brought into relation to God. The life of faith does not consist of acts of worship or of great self-denial and heroic virtues, but of all the daily conscious acts of our lives.

Human Wits Versus Divine Wisdom
Genesis 31: 21

Jacob, of all the Bible characters, ever remains the best example of the recipient of God's life and power, simply because of the appalling mixture of the good and the bad, the noble and ignoble, in him. His towering nobility is never far to seek in the midst of all his abominations. We have the notion that it is only when we are pure and right and holy that God will appear to us; also we are apt to say that God's blessing is a sign that we are right with Him.

After Surrender, What?
Matthew 11: 28; 16: 24

Has Jesus Christ saved you by His sovereign grace? Has He given you His rest? If He has not, there is no use praying about it, there is only one thing to do—come to Him and take it. Or has Jesus Christ been trying to get you to surrender yourself to be a disciple of His? He brought you to the point long ago but you baulked it again and again. Or is it a question of being united with the death of Jesus until nothing ever appeals to you that did not appeal to Him?

After surrender—what? The whole of the life after surrender is an aspiration, an aspiration after unbroken communion with God.

The Snare of Superstition

Genesis 31: 34

A mascot is a talisman of some sort whose presence is supposed to bring good luck. The persistence of the superstitious element is one of the most indelible stains on the character of otherwise good people, and it abounds in our own day. A reawakening of superstition always follows on the heels of gross materialism in either personal or national life. When once the 'mascot' tendency is allowed in the temple of the Holy Ghost, spiritual muddle-headedness is sure to result. Beware of excusing spiritual muddle-headedness in yourself, if it is not produced by the 'Jacob' reserve, it is produced by the 'Rachel' wit, and the only way out of the muddle is to walk in the light as God is in the light.

Christian Love in Action

1 Corinthians 13: 4-7

Love is the sovereign preference of my person for another person, and Jesus demands that that other Person be Himself; and the direction of Divine living is that I deliberately identify myself with Jesus Christ's interests in other people. "Love suffereth long, and is kind; love envieth not; love seeketh not its own, is not provoked, taketh not account of evil, beareth all things, believeth all things, hopeth all things, endureth all things. Love never faileth." That is Christian living in actual life. If I have the disposition of a fault-finder, I am a most uncomfortable person to live with, but if the love of God has been shed abroad in my heart, I begin to see extraordinary self-sacrifice under the roughest of exteriors.

The Test of Spiritual Education

2 *Peter* 1: 5–7

Am I getting nobler, better, more helpful, more humble, as I get older? Am I exhibiting the life that men take knowledge of as having been with Jesus, or am I getting more self-assertive, more deliberately determined to have my own way? It is a great thing to tell yourself the truth.

These are some of the lines of spiritual education: learning the dimensions of Divine Love, that the centre of that love is holiness; that the direction of Divine living is a deliberate surrender of our own point of view in order to learn Jesus Christ's point of view, and seeing that men and women are nourished in the knowledge of Jesus. The only way that can be done is by being loyal to Jesus myself.

The Cross, Revealing the Love of a Holy God

1 *John* 4: 10

In the Cross we may see the dimensions of Divine love. The Cross is not the cross of a man, but the exhibition of the heart of God. At the back of the wall of the world stands God with His arms outstretched, and every man driven there is driven into the arms of God. The Cross of Jesus is the supreme evidence of the love of God (Romans 8: 35–9). "Who shall separate us from the love of Christ?" (v. 35).

The Cross of Christ reveals that the blazing centre of the love of God is the holiness of God, not His kindness and compassion. If the Divine love pretends I am all right when I am all wrong, then I have a keener sense of justice than the Almighty. God is a holy God, and the marvel of the Redemption is that God the Holy One puts into me, the unholy one, a new disposition, the disposition of His Son.

Not Consecration But Concentration
Ezekiel 8: 1

". . . as I sat in mine house, the hand of the Lord God fell there upon me." Ezekiel's abstraction is typical of spiritual concentration —shut out from external things for concentration on the purpose of God. The great need for Christians to-day is occasional fasting from intellectual and religious and social activities in order to give ourselves wholly to the realization of some purpose of God. Acts of consecration and devotional exercises leave us much the same; concentration on God never leaves us the same. This place is for concentration on God and on nothing else.

A Prophet's Portrait of Christ
Isaiah 53

If you want to know the characterization of the Person of Christ you will find it here, sketched by His Father, through the mouth of Isaiah. The prophet Isaiah, more even than the Apostle Paul, interprets the Person of Christ; his is the power of seeing not with the outward eye, but with the inward vision of the spirit. In these latter chapters an alteration comes over Isaiah's picturing of the Servant of Jehovah; it is no longer a personification, but a Person; the great truth dawns on the prophet that it is God Himself in His Servant who is the Redeemer of His people.

'Despised and Rejected'

Isaiah 53: 3

When Our Lord came on this earth how many discerned Him? "We needs must love the Highest when we see it;" but the highest is measured by our inner disposition, and when the Son of God, who was The Highest, appeared, men did not love Him; in fact, He was unheeded, despised and rejected. He could easily be unheeded because He did not resent it; He could be treated like the earth under our feet. If we belong to His crowd we shall be despised. Watch how people treat you who don't love Him.

Preaching Christ Crucified

1 Corinthians 2: 2

"He was despised, and we esteemed Him not." This is God's picture of how His Servant will appear, not sometimes, but at all times. We will preach what the apostle Paul never preached; we will preach an exalted Christ: Paul said, "For I determined not to know anything among you, save Jesus Christ and Him *crucified*." Modern holiness teachers ignore God's method and present what is called the glory side; we have to present the side represented by the Cross. These are all characteristics of this implicit difference; we say, "Surely God does not mean we have to present a despised and neglected and crucified Jesus?" He does.

August 24th

Vicarious Suffering, Realized

Isaiah 53: 4

The coming of God is always on the line where the devil and sin have ranged themselves—"But where sin abounded, grace did much more abound." The majority of people who have never been touched by affliction see Jesus Christ's death as a thing beside the mark; but when a man is convicted of sin, then for the first time he begins to see something else—"At last I see; I thought He was smitted *of God*; but now I see He was wounded for *my* transgressions. He was bruised for *my* iniquities: the chastisement of *my* peace was upon Him."

August 25th

'Not Offended in Me'

Matthew 11: 6

We have the idea that prosperity, or happiness, or morality, is the end of a man's existence; according to the Bible it is something other, viz., "to glorify God and enjoy Him for ever." When a man is right with God, God puts His honour in that man's keeping. Job is one of those in whom God has staked His honour, and it was during the process of His inexplicable ways that Job makes his appeal for mercy, and yet all through there comes out his implicit confidence in God. "And blessed is he, whosoever shall not be offended in Me," said Our Lord.

The Trial of Your Faith

1 Peter 1: 7

The nature of faith is that it must be tested; and the trial of faith does not come in fits and starts, it goes on all the time. The one thing that keeps us right with God is the great work of His grace in our hearts. All the prophets had to take part in something they did not understand, and the Christian has to do the same. If we were to say "This is the way God is going to work," it would lead to spiritual pride, to the ban of finality about our views, to imagining that God was on our side. The question for us is, will we so yield ourselves wholly to the realization of some purpose of God? 'The trial of your faith' is in order to bring God into the practical details of your life.

Not a Circle But a Cross

2 Corinthians 5: 18, 19

When the Bible speaks of the Death of Jesus it is not as the crucifixion of a Nazarene Carpenter, but as the point in history which reveals the nature of God—that He is not sitting on the remote circle of the world in omnipotent indifference, but that He is right at the very heart of things. The symbol for God is not a circle, but a cross, symbolic of supreme suffering and distress.

The Meaning and Cost of Forgiveness

Isaiah 53: 7–11

Forgiveness of sin is the great revelation of God, all the rest is slight. We have belittled the meaning of forgiveness of *sin* by making it mean the forgiveness of offences. The only way God can forgive sin is because His Servant 'poured out His soul unto death.' Have I ever realized that the only way I am forgiven is by the panging depth of suffering God's Servant went through? The consciousness of what sin is comes long after the redemptive processes have been at work. The man who comes to for God for the first time convicted of sins knows nothing about sin; it is the ripest saint who knows what sin is. Our salvation is the outcome of what it cost the Son of God. "He shall see of the travail of His soul, and shall be satisfied."

A Voice Brings Peace

John 6: 19, 20

Children are sometimes afraid in the dark, fear gets into their hearts and nerves and they get into a tremendous state; then they hear the voice of mother or father and all is quietened and they go off to sleep. In our own spiritual experience it is the same, some great fear or terror comes down the road to meet us and our hearts are seized with a tremendous fear, then we hear our own name called, and the voice of Jesus saying, "It is I, be not afraid," and the peace of God which passeth all understanding takes possession of our hearts.

Forming the Mind of Christ

Luke 21: 19

"In your patience ye shall win your souls," said Jesus to His disciples. Soul is the expression of my personal spirit in my body, the way I reason and think and act, and Jesus taught that a man must lose his soul in order to gain it; he must lose absolutely his own way of reasoning and looking at things, and begin to estimate from an entirely different standpoint. We have the Spirit of Jesus gifted to us, but we have to form the mind which was also in Christ Jesus. No man has the mind of Christ unless he has acquired it.

The Discipline of Divine Loyalty

John: 21: 15-17

Is that what we have been doing, feeding Jesus Christ's sheep? Take a rapid survey—have we been nourishing the lives of people in the understanding of Jesus, or has our aim been to maintain our particular deposit of doctrine? "Divine loyalty," says Jesus, "is that you feed My sheep in the knowledge of Me, not feed them with your doctrine." Peter had boasted earlier of his love for Jesus— "though all men shall be offended because of Thee, yet will I never be offended," but there is no brag left in him now—"Lord, Thou knowest all things; Thou knowest that I love Thee." "Feed My sheep." The discipline of Divine loyalty is not that I am true to a doctrine, but so true to Jesus that other people are nourished in the knowledge of Him. Get rid of the idea that you must do good things, and remember what Jesus says, "If you believe on Me, out of you will flow rivers of living water." In the Christian life it is never "Do, do," but "Be, be, and I will do through you." The type of man produced by the Spirit of Jesus is the one who bears a growing family likeness to Jesus.

September 1st

Spiritual Maturity

Luke 3: 23

"Being about thirty years of age . . ."—the period of maturity. Who reached maturity? The Son of God as Man, the maturity of all physical powers, all soul powers, all spiritual powers, and not until that point was reached did God thrust Him out into the three years of service. "I do always those things that are pleasing to My Father." Where did Jesus learn that power? In those thirty silent years.

Can God say of us—"That soul is learning, line upon line, precept upon precept; it is not nearly so petulant and stupid as it used to be, it no longer sulks in corners, it no longer murmurs against discipline, it is getting slowly to the place where I shall be able to do with it what I did with My own Son?"

September 2nd

Spiritual Freedom

John 14: 23

"If a man love Me, . . . he will keep My word," said Jesus; He is referring to the freedom of the disciple to keep His commandments. No natural man is free to keep the commandments of God, he is utterly unable to unless he is born again of the Holy Spirit. Freedom means ability to keep the law; every kind of freedom has to be earned. "And My Father will love him, and We will come unto him, and make Our abode with him"—an unspeakable, unstateable communion, God the Father, God the Son and God the Holy Ghost, and the sinner saved and sanctified by grace, communing together.

His Life Laid Down, and Ours

John 10: 17, 18

"I lay it down of Myself" (John 10: 17–18). Our Lord is referring to the power He has of Self-sacrifice. Have we that power? Thank God we have. After sanctification we have the power to deliberately take our sanctified selves and sacrifice them for God. It is an easy business to be self-sacrificing in mind—"I intend to do this and that," that is, I estimate what it is going to cost me. Paul says he not only estimated the cost, he experienced it. ". . . for Whom I suffered the loss of all things." As you go on towards maturity watch the by-path meadows—"I have been so blessed of God here, this is where I ought to stay." Read the life of Jesus, He kept His eye fixed on the one purpose His Father had for His life, which He calls 'going up to Jerusalem,' and we have to go with Him there.

'By All Means to Save Some'

1 Corinthians 9: 22

A worker for God must be prepared to endure hardness; he must learn how to 'sop up' all the bad and turn it into good, and nothing but the supernatural grace of God and his sense of obligation will enable him to do it. As workers will be brought into relationship with people for whom we have no affinity; we have to stand for one thing only, "That I might by all means save some." The one mastering obligation of our life as a worker is to persuade men for Jesus Christ, and to do that we have to learn to live among facts: the fact of human stuff as it is, not as it ought to be; and the fact of Bible revelation, whether it agrees with our doctrines or not.

Are We True Prophets?

Jeremiah 23: 9

In chapter 23 Jeremiah speaks against the accredited leaders of the day and against the professional preachers. All that refers to the prophets of the Old Testament dispensation has a direct application to us, no matter what we think we are. The principles are for all, even the most insignificant of us. A great deal of what we proclaim can never be worked out in experience, but whenever a standard has to be proclaimed we are exonerated or condemned according to the way we carry out those dictates of the Spirit of God. We must be the living incarnation of what we teach or else we are humbugs.

The Wonder of the Child

Luke 2: 49

"How is it that ye sought Me? wist ye not that I must be in My Father's house?" (v. 49). This incident is the one glimpse given to us of those twelve years so full of wonder, so full of sky-lights open towards God. Think of the pure wonder of the Child Jesus in the temple when He realized with spiritual intuition that He was in His Father's House; don't picture a precocious intellectual prig, Jesus was amazed that His Mother did not know what He knew, or understand what He understood. A child's mind exhibits the innocence of intelligence, and in the life of Jesus this innocence never became conceited.

September 7th

The Value of the Waiting Time
Luke 2: 51

"And He was subject unto them" (v. 51). Have we ever caught the full force of the thirty silent years, of those three years wandering in Palestine? Have we ever caught the full force of those ten days of waiting in the upper room? If we measure those periods by our modern way of estimating we will put it down as waste of time; but into the life of Our Lord, into the lives of the early disciples, were going to come elements that would root and ground them on a solid foundation that nothing could shake. The waiting time is always the testing time.

September 8th

The Saints' Reaction to Suffering
2 Corinthians 4: 16, 17

The evident indifference on the part of the saints in the New Testament, and since, to the experience of suffering is accounted for, not on the ground of insensitiveness or by tramping on the finer feelings, but by the 'expulsive power of a new affection.' When we are saved and sanctified through the Atonement we are led out into the fulfilment of the ideas of God under the Lordship of Jesus Christ. Every other aim falls into insignificance and through earth's heart-breaks, sorrows and griefs, the sanctified soul treads calm and un-wavering, unafraid even of death itself, summing up all as 'our light affliction, which is for the moment . . .'

The Peril of Reformation

Luke 11: 24

Luke 11: 24 is a picture of clear sweeping reformation, the house 'swept and garnished'; but our Lord is pointing out in the parable the peril of a moral victory un-used because the heart is left empty. The man who reforms without any knowledge of the grace of God is the subtlest infidel with regard to the need of regeneration. It is a good thing to have the heart swept, but it becomes the worst thing if the heart is left vacant for spirits more evil than itself to enter; Jesus says that "the last state of that man becometh worse than the first." Reformation is a good thing, but like every other good thing it is the enemy of the best. Regeneration means filling the heart with something positive, viz., the Holy Spirit (Luke 11: 13).

Remorse Not Repentance

Genesis 4: 9–14
(also Matthew 27: 5)

Never mistake remorse for repentance; remorse simply puts a man in hell while he is on earth, it carries no remedial quality with it at all, nothing that betters a man. An unawakened sinner has no remorse, but immediately a man recognizes his sin he experiences the pain of being gnawed by a sense of guilt, for which punishment would be a heaven of relief, but no punishment can touch it. In the case of Cain (*see* Genesis 4: 9–14) remorse is seen at its height: "Mine iniquity is greater than can be forgiven" (v. 13, R.V. marg.). Cain was in the condition of being found out by his own sin; his conscience recognized what he had done, and he knew that God recognized it too.

September 11th

Expansion Demands Expression

Philippians 2: 12, 13

When God gives a vision of what sanctification means, or what the life of faith means, we have instantly to pay for the vision, and we pay for it by the inevitable law that 'expansion must be followed by concentration.' That means we must concentrate on the vision until it becomes real. Over and over again the vision is mistaken for the reality. God's great Divine anticipation can only be made manifest by our human participation, these two must not be put asunder. Every expansion of brain and heart that God gives in meetings or in private reading of the Bible must be paid for inevitably and inexorably by concentration on our part, not by consecration. God will continually bring us into circumstances to make us prove whether we will work out with determined concentration what He has worked in.

September 12th

Faith Claims the Whole Man

Hebrews 11: 6

Faith is not a faculty, faith is the whole man rightly related to God by the power of the Spirit of Jesus. We are apt to apply faith to certain domains of our lives only, e.g., we have faith in God when we ask Him to save us, or ask Him for the Holy Spirit, but we trust something other than God in the actual details of our lives. "Faith claims the whole man and all that God's grace can make him," just as it claimed the whole of our Lord's life. Our Lord represents the normal man, not the average man, but the man according to God's norm; His life was not cut up into compartments, one part sacred and another secular, it was not in any way a mutilated life. Jesus Christ was concentrated on one line, viz., the will of His Father, in every detail of His life.

Under Divine Orders

1 Corinthians 3: 23; John 13: 13

If for one whole day, quietly and determinedly, we were to give ourselves up to the ownership of Jesus and to obeying His orders, we should be amazed at its close to realize all He had packed into that one day. We say—"Oh, but I have a special work to do." No Christian has a special work to do. A Christian is called to be Jesus Christ's own, one chosen by Him; one who is not above his Master, and who does not dictate to Jesus as to what he intends to do. Our Lord calls to no special work; He calls to Himself. Pray to the Lord of the harvest, and He will engineer your circumstances and thrust you out.

The Missionary's Secret

Acts 26: 16-18

The great Author and Originator of all missionary enterprise is God, and we must keep in touch with His line. The call to the missionary does not arise out of the discernment of his own mind, or from the sympathy of his own heart, but because behind the face of every downtrodden heathen, he sees the face of Jesus Christ, and hears His command—"Go ye therefore, and make disciples of all the nations." The need of the heathen world can only be met by our Risen Lord who has all power in heaven and in earth, and by our receiving from Him the enduement of power from on high.

Going Up to Jerusalem

Luke 9: 51

The New Testament centres round one Person, the Lord Jesus Christ. We are regenerated into His Kingdom by means of His Cross, and then we go up to our Jerusalem, having His Life as our example. We must be born from above before we can go up to our Jerusalem, and the things He met with on His way will throw a flood of light on the things we shall meet with. Our Jerusalem means the place where we reach the climax of Our Lord's will for us, which is that we may be made one with Him as He is one with the Father.

The Passion of the Sanctified

1 Thessalonians 5: 23

A child in the natural world is not fit for life unless it is perfectly healthy; sanctification is spiritual health, 'perfect soundness.' May the God of peace sanctify us wholly so that we are no longer sickly souls retarding His purposes, but 'perfected through suffering.' Oh, that from every heart may rise the yearning longing as from the Apostle Paul:

> Then as I weary me and long and languish,
>   Nowise availing from that pain to part,—
> Desperate tides of the whole great world's anguish
>   Forced thro' the channels of a single heart.
>
> Oh to save these! to perish for their saving,
>   Die for their life, be offered for them all!

The Upward Look

Psalm 121: 1

Psalm 121: 1 portrays well the upward look—"Shall I lift up mine eyes to the hills? from whence should my help come? My help cometh from the Lord, which made heaven and earth." The upward look of a mature man of God is not to the mountains which God has made, but to the God who made the mountains. It is the maintained set of the highest powers of a man—not stargazing till you stumble, but the upward gaze deliberately set towards God. He has got through the 'choppy waters' of his elementary spiritual experience and now he is set on God; but you have to fight for it. "I have set the Lord always before me," said the Psalmist. Our Lord presents the upward look to the last degree of perfection.

The Forward Look

Isaiah 33: 17

"Thine eyes shall see the king in His beauty: they shall behold a far stretching land"—("a land of far distances," marg.) (Isaiah 33: 17). The forward look is the look that sees everything in God's perspective whereby His wonderful distance is put on the things that are nearest. Caleb had the perspective of God; the men who went up with him saw only the inhabitants as giants and themselves as grasshoppers. Learn to take the long view and you will breathe the benediction of God among the squalid things that surround you. Some people never get ordinary or commonplace, they transfigure everything they touch because they have got the forward look which brings confidence in God into their actual life.

Human Nature and Holiness

Romans 6: 12–19

When I am born again my human nature is not different, it is the same as before; I am related to life in the same way, I have the same bodily organs, but the mainspring is different, and I have to see now that I am dominated by the new disposition (*see* Romans 6: 13, 19). You cannot live the life God wants you to live as a saint unless you remain the man or woman God meant you to be. There is only one kind of human nature, and that is the human nature we have all got; there is only one kind of holiness, and that is the holiness of Jesus Christ. Give Him 'elbow room,' and He will manifest Himself in you, and other people will recognize Him.

Offended With Jesus?

John 6: 66

. . . "From that time many of His disciples went back, and walked no more with Him." The crowds have passed now, you are alone with your Lord, and He bends through the gloom of your weakness and blindness and says "You are not going away too, are you?"

Men are still offended at Jesus; they hear gladly His 'Follow Me' and enthusiastically leave all to follow, but when the way becomes narrow, and to follow costs shedding of blood, they begin to waver. As long as it means peace and joy we will follow Jesus, but when it costs us dear we are tempted to go back and walk no more with Him.

The Power of the Blood

John 6: 53–56

'Blood' is an offence not only at the beginning of the Christian career, but in the midst of it. "Except ye eat the flesh of the Son of Man, and drink His blood, ye have no life in you." . . . "Doth this offend you?" said Jesus—"Except you are crucified with Christ until all that is left is the life of Christ in your flesh and blood, *you have no life in you*." "Except your self-love is flooded away by the inrush of the love of Jesus so that you feel your blood move through you in tender charity as it moved through Him, *you have no life in you*." "Except your flesh becomes the temple of His holiness and you abide in Christ and He in you, *you have no life in you*."

The Sentence of Death

2 Corinthians 1: 9

If I am in fellowship with Jesus Christ and am indwelt by Him, I have the answer of death in myself, and nothing the world, the flesh or the devil can do can touch me. This divine light came to Paul out of his desperate experience in Ephesus; he realized then that nothing could any more affright him. The discipline of fellowship brought about in Paul's experience the assimilation of what he believed. We say many things which we believe, but they have never been tested. Discipline has to come through all the things we believe in order to turn them into real spiritual possessions. It is the trial of our faith that is precious. 'Hang in' to Jesus Christ against all odds until He turns your spiritual beliefs into real possessions. It is heroism to believe in God.

September 23rd

Jesus Understands the Power of Our Enemy

Luke 22: 31, 32

Peter loved Jesus Christ and declared that he was ready to lay down his life for Him, and yet he denied Him thrice with oaths and curses. But Jesus never lost heart over him, He told him beforehand —". . . but I made supplication for thee, that thy faith fail not: and do thou, when once thou hast turned again, stablish thy brethren." Sin never once frightened Jesus; the devil never once frightened Him. Face Jesus Christ with all the power of the devil: "He was manifested, that He might *destroy the works of the devil.*" Are you being tripped up by the subtle power of the devil? Remember, Jesus Christ has power not only to release you, but to make you more than conqueror over all the devil's onslaughts.

September 24th

More Than a Sympathizer, a Saviour

Luke 4: 17–19

To picture Jesus Christ, never so beautifully, as One who sits down beside the broken-hearted and by expression of fellow-feeling and overflowing tenderness, enables him to be resigned and submissive to his lot, is not only thoroughly to misunderstand our Lord, but to prevent Him doing what He came to do. He does come to the broken-hearted, to the captives bound by a cursed hereditary tendency, to the blind who grope for light, to the man bruised and crushed by his surroundings, but He does not come as a sympathizer —He "binds up the broken-hearted, gives release to the captives, recovering of sight to the blind; He sets at liberty them that are bruised." Jesus Christ is not a mere sympathizer, He is a Saviour, and the only One.

The Altar of Fellowship

2 Corinthians 12: 15

Human fellowship can go to great lengths, but not all the way. Fellowship with God can go all lengths. The Apostle Paul literally fulfilled what we mean by this phrase, the altar of fellowship; he offered himself liberally and freely to God, and then offered himself at the hands of God, freely and fully, for the service of God among men, whether or not men understood him. "And I will very gladly spend and be spent for you; though the more abundantly I love you, the less I be loved." Do we know anything about this altar of fellowship whereby we offer back to God the best He has given us, and then let Him re-offer it as broken bread and poured-out wine to His other children?

Prayer on the Right Basis

Acts 4: 31

How strongly spiritual efficacy in prayer is marked all through the Acts of the Apostles! It is the sign Jesus Christ gives that we believe in Him (*see* John 14: 12-13). Prayer that is not saturated in the New Testament is apt to be based on human earnestness. God never hears prayer because a man is in earnest; He hears and answers prayer that is on the right platform—we have "boldness to enter into the holy place *by the blood of Jesus*," and by no other way. It is not our agony and our distress, but our childlike confidence in God.

The Liberated Preacher

Acts 5: 20

Unless a preacher has had a saving experience, i.e., been set free from some 'prison,' he has not got God's 'go' in him. If this test were put to every preacher and Sunday School teacher—Has Jesus Christ done anything for you you could not do for yourself? has He set you free from the 'prison' of a wrong disposition, set you free from the tyranny of nerves? from pride? from a wrong mental outlook? —the result straightaway would be to thin the number of those who are at work for God, and those that were left would be the men of God's method. The man of God's method says—"I know I have been delivered by God; I don't know *how* He did it, but I know He did it."

Christ's Knowledge of the Human Heart

Matthew 15: 19

Jesus Christ treated men from the standpoint of His certain knowledge of them; He is the supreme Master of the human heart. Recall what He said—"for from within, out of the heart of man, proceed . . . ," consequently He was never surprised, never in a panic. When He met the rich young ruler, an upright-living splendid young man, we read that "Jesus looking upon him loved him." Jesus Christ loved morality, but He never said it was enough. "If thou wilt be perfect . . ." then come the conditions, Jesus knew that at the back of the natural virtues was a disposition that could wilfully sin against God. Again when He met Nicodemus, a godly man, a ruler of the synagogue, He told him he must be made all over again before he could enter the kingdom of God.

September 29th

"Having Done All, to Stand"

Ephesians 6: 13

". . . and stand." It takes a tremendously strong man to stand—
"and, having done all, to stand" (Ephesians 6: 18). Not fight, but
stand. The men of God's method are never hustled, never enticed,
they won't allow themselves to be deflected, they know what they
are there for. "None of these things move me," said Paul, "you may
execrate me, or praise me, it makes no difference; I am here for only
one thing—to fufil the ministry which I received from the Lord
Jesus."

September 30th

What Do You Know?

John 13: 3, 4

"Jesus knowing . . . that He was come from God . . ."

Do you know that you have received the Holy Spirit, know that
you are a child of God—are you going to be greater than Jesus
Christ? Are you going to be disdainful—"What a humiliating thing
to do!" Jesus, knowing who He was, took a towel and washed the
disciples' feet; and He says, "I have given you an example, that ye
should do as I have done to you." To shout 'Hallelujah' is humbug
unless it is genuine. Jesus never tells you to shout 'Hallelujah':
He says—"*Do as I have done to you.*" How much long-suffering
mercy has God shown you?

The Witness of Sorrow

Ezekiel 9: 11

In this ancient Book of Ezekiel the man clothed in linen, with a writer's inkhorn by his side, was to set a mark upon the foreheads of the men who sorrowed for the city's sin. Let us take time to wonder if such a visitant on such an errand would mark us as among the people privileged to sorrow thus. Jeremiah has been called 'the weeping prophet,' and in his Lamentations we find that the secret of his sorrow is Jerusalem, the city of his love. "How doth the city sit solitary, that was full of people!" (1: 1.) Instantly our minds pass on to what is recorded in Luke 19: 41, "And when He drew nigh, He saw the city and wept over it," and we remember with adoring wonder that Our Lord is known throughout all generations as 'a Man of sorrows.'

Worldly Sorrow

2 Corinthians 7: 10

It is a terrible thing to say, and yet true, that there is a sorrow so selfish, so sentimental and sarcastic that it adds to the sin of the city. All sorrow that arises from being baffled in some selfish aim of our own is of the world and works death. Those who sorrow over their own weaknesses and sins and stop short at that, have a sorrow that only makes them worse, it is not a godly sorrow that works repentance. Oh that all men knew that every sentiment has its appropriate reaction, and if the nature does not embrace that reaction it degenerates into a sullen sentimentalism that kills all good action.

Fruitful Sorrow

Lamentations 1: 12

The sign for the world without God is a circle, complete in and for itself; the sign for the Christian is the Cross. The Christian knows by bitter yet blessed conviction of sin that no man is sufficient for himself, and he thereby enters into identification with the Cross of Calvary, and he longs and prays and works to see the sinful, self-centred world broken up and made the occasion for the mighty Cross to have its way whereby men may come to God and God come down to men.

Failure in Sorrow

Matthew 26: 40; 1 Corinthians 11: 30

There are many to-day who are suffering from spiritual sleeping sickness, and the sorrow of the world which works death is witnessed in all directions. If personal sorrow does not work itself out along the appropriate line, it will lull us to a pessimistic sleep. For instance, when we see our brother 'sinning a sin not unto death' do we get to prayer for him, probed by the searching sorrow of his sin? (*see* 1 John 5: 16).

No Second Causes

John 19: 11

We are too shallow to be afraid of God. All the Hebrew prophets reveal this truth, that there is only one Cause and no 'second causes.' It requires a miracle of grace before we believe this, consequently we are foolishly fearless, but when the grace of God lifts us into the life of God we fear nothing and no one saving God alone. The 'no second causes' truth was ever apparent to Our Lord, e.g., "Thou couldest have no power at all against Me, except it were given thee from above."

God's Inexorable Demands

Hebrews 12: 14

If my first step has not been one of penitential repentance I will at one time meet the 'artillery' of God and down I go, no matter how earnestly I pray and mouth my testimony, for this reason—God will have nothing in His Presence but holiness and uprightness and integrity. "Those things will never happen to me, there are circumstances in my case which exonerate," there are not. God's demands are inexorable, only one thing will satisfy Him, and that is speckless, spotless holiness, and He will never let us go until He has brought us there—unless we wrest ourselves out of His hand.

October 7th

The Only Way

John 14: 6

"I am the Way"—God has no other Way. Jesus Christ is the only Way in every profound problem, the reason we can do without Him is that we have not come up against profound things. We may have a vivid religious experience and yet not think along Christian lines. All things are not black or white, right or wrong; there is no problem about right and wrong, these things are clearly marked; but there are things that are perplexing, is Jesus Christ 'the Way' in those? We are apt to get impatient with the things that are obscure and difficult to decipher.

October 8th

All Things . . . to the Lord

Colossians 3: 23

If there is anything in my life in which I have to justify myself, I am not walking in the light.

Beware of being negligent in some lesser thing while being good in a greater thing, e.g. I may be good in a prayer meeting but not good in the matter of cleaning my boots. It is a real peril, and springs from selecting some one thing our Lord taught as our standard instead of God Himself.

The Lion Lamb

Revelation 5: 8

In the days of His flesh Jesus Christ exhibited this Divine paradox of the Lion and the Lamb—He was the Lion in majesty, rebuking winds and demons: He was the Lamb in meekness, "who when He was reviled, reviled not again." He was the Lion in power, raising Lazarus and others from the dead: He was the Lamb in patience, who was "brought as a lamb to the slaughter, and as a sheep before her shearers is dumb, so He openeth not his mouth." He was the Lion in authority—"Ye have heard that it was said, . . . but *I* say unto you . . .:" He was the Lamb in gentleness, taking little children up in His arms and saying "Suffer little children, and forbid them not, to come unto Me."

The Vine—for Fruit or Fire

John 15: 5, 6

The vine is of no value if it is not fruitful; trees which are not fruit-bearing are excellent for other purposes, but not so the vine which is fit only for fruit or for fire. What God burns is not weakness, not imperfection, but perverted goodness. Fruit is the manifestation of the essential nature of the tree, and our human lives are meant to bring forth the fruit of the Spirit, which is, literally, the life of God in me, invading me, producing fruit for His glory. "Herein is My Father glorified, that ye bear much fruit."

The Divine Withdrawal

Song of Songs 5: 6

Interior desolation serves a vital purpose in the life of a Christian. At the beginning of the spiritual life the consciousness of God is so wonderful that we are apt to imagine our communion with God depends upon our being conscious of His presence. Then when God begins to withdraw us into Himself and things become mysterious, we lose our faith and get into the dark, and say—"I must have backslidden," and yet we know we have not, all we know is that we have lost our consciousness of God's presence.

Making the Natural Spiritual

1 Corinthians 6: 19

Every part of our human nature which is not brought into subjection to the Holy Spirit after experiencing deliverance from sin will prove a corrupting influence. We are not delivered from human nature; human nature was created by God, not by the devil; it is impaired, and enfeebled, but it is not sinful. The first creation retains the remnants of God's handiwork; re-creation is the building of a spiritual habitation, 'an habitation of God,' and all our effort is to be spent in disciplining the natural life in obedience to the new creation wrought in us through the Spirit. If I refuse to make my natural life spiritual by the slow process of obedience, my religious profession becomes a disgusting hypocrisy.

Climate and Character
Mark 4: 39

The life of Our Lord exhibits the influence of character on climate. It is easy to make this absurd, but looked at from the attitude of the Spirit of God you find there is an amazing connection between the storm and distresses and wild confusion of the earth just now and the waywardness and wrong of man; when the waywardness of man ceases and the sons of God are manifested then "the creature itself also shall be delivered from the bondage of corruption into the glorious liberty of the children of God."

October 14th

Communion at Daybreak
Luke 6: 12, 13

It is not a haphazard thing, but in the constitution of God, that there are certain times of the day when it not only seems easier, but it *is* easier, to meet God. If you have ever prayed in the dawn you will ask yourself why you were so foolish as not to do it always. It is difficult to get into communion with God in the midst of the hurly-burly of the day. It is not sentiment but an implicit reality that the conditions of dawn and communion with God go together. When the day of God appears there will be no night, always dawn and day. There is nothing of the nature of strain in God's Day, it is all free and beautiful and fine.

The Source and the Outflow

John 7: 38

Jesus did not say, "He that believeth on Me, shall experience the fulness of the blessing of God"; but, "he that believeth on Me, out of him shall escape everything he receives." It is a picture of the unfathomable, incalculable benediction which will flow from the one great sovereign Source, belief in Jesus. We have nothing to do with the outflow; we have to see to it that we are destitute enough of spiritual independence to be filled with the Holy Ghost and then pay attention to the Source Our Lord Himself. You can never measure what God will do through you if you are rightly related to Jesus. The parenthesis in v. 39 does not apply to us: the Holy Ghost *has been* given; Jesus *is* glorified; the rivers of living water are there, and, unspeakable wonder! the sacrament may flow through our lives too. All that the one out of whom the rivers of living water are flowing is conscious of is belief in Jesus and maintaining a right relationship to Him; then day by day God is pouring the rivers of living water through you, and it is of His mercy He does not let you know it.

Wrath or Love?

Romans 2: 5; 8: 28

When our supreme temptation comes, the setting we are in, whether it is a city or the actual desert, brings us into contact with the foundation of things as God made them. According to Genesis, the basis of physical material life is chaos, and the basis of personal moral life, wrath. If I live in harmony with God, chaos becomes cosmos to me, and the wrath of God becomes the love of God. If I get out of touch with God I get into hell, physically and morally; when I live in relationship to God by the inner witness of the Spirit "Heaven above is brighter blue, earth around a sweeter green . . ."

The Desperation of a Disciple

Luke 22: 31, 32

The devil tried to get Peter where he got Judas, but he did not succeed; Satan did not 'enter into' Peter; Peter got the length of denying Jesus, but in his wilderness of temptation he 'struck' the Divine; consequently Peter experienced a desperation producing tears, and those tears were the most amazing bitterness in his life. Peter with his impulsive heart would feel he could never forgive himself, he would have spent the rest of his days mourning, but Jesus had told him beforehand, "And do thou, when once thou hast turned again, establish thy brethren."

God's Love in Our Hearts

John 17: 26

Recall to your mind the touchings of the love of God in your life, and you will never find it difficult to do anything He says. It is not your power of loving God that enables you to do it, it is the presence of the very nature of God in your heart that makes it so easy to obey Him that you don't know you are obeying Him. Never quench that spirit.

A Deserved Rebuke

Mark 4: 40

Our Lord rebuked the desciples for fearing when apparently they had good reason for being alarmed. The problem is—if Jesus Christ is only the Carpenter of Nazareth, then the disciples were foolish to put Him at the tiller; but if He is the Son of God, what are they alarmed about? If Jesus Christ is God, where is my trust in Him? If He is not God, why am I so foolish as to pretend to worship Him? "And they feared exceedingly, and said one to another, What manner of man is this, that even the wind and the sea obey Him?"

Faith Tested in the Storm

Psalm 46: 2, 3

God engineers us out of the sequestered places and brings us into elemental conditions and we get a taste of what the world is like because of the disobedience of man. We realize then that our hold on God has been a civilized hold, we have not really believed in Him at all. When we get out on to the deep and the darkness we realize what a wonderful thing the Psalmist says—"Therefore will we not fear, though the earth be removed . . ." But it takes some confidence in God to say that when everything you trust in has gone.

Confidence Amid World Trouble

Mark 13: 7

Jesus Christ teaches us to build our confidence in the abiding reality of Himself in the midst of everything. If a man puts his confidence in the things which must go, imagine his incomprehensible perplexity when they do go. No wonder Jesus said "men's hearts fail in them for fear." These words describe the time we are in now. But to His desciples Jesus said, "When *you* hear of wars and rumours of wars, see that ye be not troubled." Our true life is not in the things which are passing, and if we build ourselves on God and His word, when they go, the marvel is that we are not scared. The thing to examine spiritually is, am I connected with Jesus Christ personally?

The Evangel More Than Ethics

Matthew 5: 48

Wherever Christianity has ceased to be vigorous it is because it has become Christian *ethics* instead of the Christian *evangel*. People will listen more readily to an exposition of the Sermon on the Mount than they will to the meaning of the Cross; but they forget that to preach the Sermon on the Mount apart from the Cross is to preach an impossibility. What is the good of telling me to love my enemies —and "Blessed are the pure in heart"? You may talk like that to further orders, but it does not amount to anything. Jesus Christ did not come to teach men to do any of these things—He did not come primarily to teach, He came to make a man the possessor of His own disposition, the disposition which is portrayed in the Sermon on the Mount.

The Blessing of the Unnoticed

Colossians 3: 23

If you are rightly devoted to Jesus Christ, you have reached the sublime height where no one thinks of noticing you, all that is noticed is that the power of God comes through all the time. It is along some such line as this that we are to understand the omniscience of God and human life. "I have had a wonderful call from God!" It takes Almighty God Incarnate in you to peel potatoes properly, and to wash heathen children for the glory of God. *Anyone* cannot do these things; anybody can do the shining in the sun and the sporting in the footlights, but it takes God's Incarnated Spirit to make you so absolutely humanly His that you are utterly unnoticeable.

God's Forgiveness and Ours

Matthew 6: 14

A self indwelt by Jesus becomes like Him. "Walk in love, even as Christ also loved you." Jesus has loved me to the end of all my meanness and selfishness and sin; now, He says, show that same love to others. "For if ye forgive men their trespasses, your heavenly Father will also forgive you,"—that is, I am to ask to be forgiven, not on the ground of the Atonement, but because I forgive. "But if ye forgive not men their trespasses, neither will your Father forgive your trespasses." That is hard hitting. Am I prepared to show the man who does evil to me the love God has shown to me? I have to learn to identify myself with God's interests in other people, and God's interests are never my selfish interests.

Helping Others Through the Straight Gate

Luke 13: 24

Struggle to gain the mastery over selfishness, and you will be a tremendous assistance; but if you don't overcome the tendency to spiritual sluggishness and self-indulgence, you are a hindrance to all around you. These things are intangible, but they are there, and Jesus says to us, "Strive to enter in at the strait gate." You never get through alone. If you struggle to get through, others are the stronger and better for knowing you. The men and women who lift and inspire us are those who struggle for self, not for self-assertiveness, that is a sign of weakness, but for the development of personality. There are some people in whose company you cannot have a mean thought without being instantly rebuked.

God's In-working and Our Out-working

Philippians 2: 12, 13

"O wretched man that I am! who shall deliver me from this chronic incapacity? I consent that a thing is right and yet I do the wrong." When the Holy Spirit comes in He energizes a man's will, He works in him to will to want to do the will of God. The deliverance is a very profound and practical one, God alters my 'want to,' i.e., the ruling disposition by introducing His own will into me. Now, says the apostle, work out your own salvation—if you are saved, exhibit it in your practical life, manifest the heavenly disposition in your home, in your business.

Defeat in the Desert

Matthew 4: 11

Jesus Christ met the devil in the wilderness and defeated Him. When you go through a time of trial, a wilderness of temptation in heart or mind or spirit, you feel inclined to get away out into somewhere like the desert. The reason for that is not haphazard, but because in the primal constitution of God man is connected with the dust of the earth. He is related to the elemental condition of things all through. When the sons of God are manifested the desolate place will alter at once. 'The desert shall rejoice, and blossom as the rose.'

Personality Split Through Sin

Romans 7: 17-25

Romans 7: is the classic for all time of the tragedy of a man whose mind is awakened by the incoming of the disturbing nature of God (*see* vv. 7-11). The incoming of the Holy Spirit into a man results sooner or later in the splitting up of personal unity into conscious conflict. There is no real spiritual stability, no spiritual triumph. Sin has so thwarted a man's personality that he has no power over it—'sold under sin'—there are things that make me do what I don't want to. The only One who can deliver him is Jesus Christ. That is the apostle's contention all through—"I thank God through Jesus Christ our Lord . . . For the law of the Spirit of life in Christ Jesus *hath made me free* from the law of sin and of death."

The Benediction of Poverty

Luke 6: 20

To-day we are so afraid of poverty that we never dream of doing anything that might involve us in being poor. We are out of the running of medieval monks who took on the vow of poverty. Many of us are poor, but none of us chooses to be. Our attitude is that if we are extravagant a rainy day will come for which we have not laid up. You cannot lay up for a rainy day and justify it in the light of Jesus Christ's teaching.

The Treasures of Darkness

Isaiah 45: 3

We often state the character of God in terms of brutal harshness which makes men atheists, while our motive is to glorify Him. Ever remember that 'eternal life' is to know God, therefore you cannot expect to know Him in five minutes or forty years. Measure your ultimate delight in God's truth and joy in God by the little bit that is clear to you. There are whole tracts of God's character unrevealed to us as yet, and we have to bow in patience until God is able to reveal the things which look so dark. The danger is lest we make the little bit of truth we do know a pinnacle on which we set ourselves to judge everyone else.

The Shadow of God's Hand

Job 13: 15, 16

One of the saddest sights is to see Christians who were true go under through the lassitude of some sorrow. This is where it begins —God brought them under the shadow of His hand, and they said, "This is the devil, I have no business to be in darkness," forgetting that there are things God cannot explain. Our Lord taught over and over again that things will never be explained in this life. We have to get rid of the idea that we are going to be vindicated down here; Jesus was not. The millennium age will be the vindication of the saints; this is the age of their humiliation.

The Divine Drawing Power

Philippians 3: 13, 14

The Calling of God means that by receiving the nature of God I am called to the goal of God Himself. A man only hears the call of a thing if he has the nature of the thing within him, and then only if he broods on it. When I am born again the nature of God is put into me and whenever God is presented I feel the draw, I cannot get away from it. "I press on," says St. Paul, "if so be that I may apprehend that for which also I was apprehended by Christ Jesus." God saves a man apart from his own working, salvation is God's 'bit' in every particular; what he has to do is to *work out* his own salvation.

November 2nd

The Cost of Spiritual Perfection

Matthew 5: 48

If I want to see the Face of God I must fast from other things and concentrate on God. If in my inner life I am under apprehension by Jesus Christ for the time being I am out of touch with ordinary things. To fast is not to give up food, but to cut off the right arm, and pluck out the right eye. But that is only a stage, what we are tending towards is the perfection Jesus speaks of in Matthew 5: 48 —"Ye therefore shall be perfect, as your heavenly Father is perfect"; but in order to get there we have to go the longest way round. The end is a relationship to God perfect and complete in every particular.

November 3rd

Joy in True Devotion

2 Corinthians 4: 7–18

Christianity is not devotion to work, or to a cause, or a doctrine, but devotion to a Person, the Lord Jesus Christ. Christianity is a personal relationship which works spontaneously by 'the moral originality of the Holy Ghost,' there is a perfect gaiety of delight. You could never awaken self-pity in the Apostle Paul, you might starve him or imprison him, but you could never knock out of him that uncrushable gaiety and certainty of God. Paul refused to take anything or anyone seriously but Jesus Christ.

Spiritual Detachment
Philippians 3: 8

"Give up your right to yourself to Me," says Jesus, "let Me realize Myself in you." He quenches the fury of desire by detaching us from things so that we may know Him. In this way God brings us into the fullness of life. The majority of us are not in the place where God can give us 'the hundredfold more.' We say, "A bird in the hand is worth two in the bush," while God is wanting to give us the bush with all the birds in it! It is necessary to be detached from things and then come back to them in a right relationship. A sense of property is a hindrance to spiritual growth, that is why so many of us know nothing about communion with Jesus Christ.

The Blessing of Affliction
Psalm 119: 67

It is a terrible truth that many of us go astray until we are afflicted (see Psalm 119: 67); we conceive in our pride that 'we shall not be moved,' and in this stage we dislike and radically disagree with the sterner presentations of God in the Bible, and it is only by the sharp sword of affliction and the profound conviction of the meanness of our pride that we are brought to see God for ourselves and are ready to turn and obey His commands.

The Danger of Disillusionment

1 Corinthians 3: 21

In spiritual life disillusionment generally comes in relation to other people, that is why Paul says, "Wherefore let no one glory in men" (1 Corinthians 3: 21) and ". . . not to think of himself more highly than he ought to think;" (Romans 12: 3). In Ezekiel 12 the disillusionment comes in connection with national life and is in relation to God: the people begin to realize that God is not what they had vainly hoped He was. Vv. 1-6 form God's answer to their expectation that He would reinstate the permanence of Jerusalem.

God's Secrets Revealed in the Dark

Deuteronomy 29: 29

There are depths inaccessible in the Divine nature; mysteries un-revealed in the method of God's procedure. God never reveals any-thing ahead of moral and spiritual progress. The Christian worker who has never walked in the darkness of God's hand with no light, has never walked with God at all. The principle of walking with God is that it is a walk by faith, not by sight; a walk in the light of Christ, not in the light of dogmatic conviction. Jesus as our example was under the shadow of the hand of God. "If it be possible, let this cup pass from Me."

The Freedom of the Father's Child

Matthew 23: 9

George MacDonald in one of his books gives a graphic description of the wonderful simplicity a child of God has; he pictures Job opening God's private door, as it were, and flinging himself into His presence and presenting his problems. He is indicating the freedom a child of God has to come and say, "I am puzzled by this and that; why should things be so?" He is coming not to a monarch who will terrify him, but to a Father, if he is a disciple, and he can speak just like a child with perfect simplicity and freedom. Some of us seem to have the idea that we are away in a howling wilderness and we must cry and agonize before we can get God's ear. Turn to the New Testament and see what Jesus says—"Father, I thank Thee that Thou hast heard Me. And I knew that Thou hearest Me always."

The Supreme Teacher

John 14: 26

The test of every spiritual impulse is, does it make Jesus Christ the supreme Teacher? Jesus said, "When the Holy Spirit is come, He shall teach you all things." The Holy Spirit is the great bond of union because He keeps us united to the one Teacher. Jesus Christ is not a great Teacher alongside Plato and other great teachers; He stands absolutely alone. "Test your teachers," said Jesus; the teachers who come from God are those who clear the way to Jesus Christ, and keep it clear. We are estimated in God's sight as workers by whether or not we clear the way for people to see Jesus.

The Blameworthy Temper

Psalm 120: 2-4

The suffering which springs from being "a meddler in other men's matters" (a busy-body) is humiliating to the last degree. A free translation of 1 Thessalonians 4: 11 might well read: "Study to shut up and mind your own business", and among all the texts we hang on our walls, let this be one. The suffering that arises from a wrong temper has no refining side, but only a humiliating one. "Therefore take heed to your spirit." A blameworthy temper of mind is the most damning thing in the human soul.

The Altar of Sacrifice

Philippians 2: 17

Paul's conception of the altar of sacrifice is 'spending and being spent' for the sake of the elementary children of God. He has no other end and aim than that—to be broken bread and poured-out wine in the hands of God that others might be nourished and fed (cf. Colossians 1: 24). The great Saviour and His great Apostle go hand-in-hand—the Son of God sacrificed Himself that men might be redeemed, Paul, the bondslave of Jesus, sacrifices himself that men might accept the Great Salvation.

November 12th

The Mind of Christ

Philippians 2: 5

When we are born again we are not given a fully formed reasoning Christian mind, we are given the Spirit of Jesus, but not His mind, we have to form that. Countless numbers of men and women are saved who never think of forming the mind of Christ. The 'mind' Paul urges these Philippian Christians to form is not the mind of Almighty God, but "the mind of Christ Jesus, who esteemed His own identity with God not a thing to be grasped at." This was the central citadel of the temptation—"You are the Son of God, then assert Your prerogative; You can bring the world to Your feet if You will only remember who You are and use Your power." The invariable answer Jesus made was, "I came not to do Mine own will though I am the Son of God; I am here in this order of things for one purpose only, to do the will of My Father."

November 13th

Where and How to Shine

Philippians 2: 15

We have to shine as lights in the squalid places of earth, we can't shine in heaven, our light would be put out in two seconds. If ever we are to be blameless, undeserving of censure in the sight of God who sees down to the motives of our motives, it must be by the supernatural power of God. That is the meaning of the Cross, that through it I can not only have God's marvellous work done in my heart, but I can have the proof of it in my life.

Are We Profaning His Holy Name?

Ezekiel 36: 20

This was the characteristic of the people of God whenever they forgot whose they were and whom they served. Under the searchlight of God we realize that God's holy Name is profaned when we put before people what God's grace has wrought in us instead of God Himself. Whenever we go into work for God from any standpoint saving that of the dominance of God, we begin to patronize at once; unless we go as the bondservants of Jesus Christ we have no business to go at all. Jesus Christ became the towel-girt Servant of His own disciples. Never deal with people from the superior person's standpoint, God never blesses that; deal only by steadily presenting the Lord Jesus Christ. The characteristic of the holiness which is the outcome of the indwelling of God is a blazing truthfulness with regard to God's word, and an amazing tenderness in personal dealing.

Happiness, a False Goal

Psalm 73: 12; Luke 12: 19

Happiness is the portion of a child, a child ought to be thoughtless and happy, and woe be to the people who upset their happiness; but if you take happiness as the end and aim for men and women you have to make its basis a determined ignorance of God, otherwise men will, like Job, 'remember God and be troubled' (Job 23: 15). Read the seventy-third Psalm, it is the description of the man who has made happiness his aim—he is not in trouble as other men, neither is he plagued like other men, he has more than heart could wish; but once let his moral equilibrium be upset by conviction of sin and all his happiness is destroyed. The coming of Jesus Christ is not a peaceful thing, but a disturbing thing, because it means the destruction of every happiness that is not based on a personal relationship to Himself.

God's Method: the Corn of Wheat

John 12: 24

This fundamental principle must ever be borne in mind—that any work for God, before it fulfils its purpose, must die, otherwise it abides alone. Outside the Bible, the conception is of progressing from a seed to full growth; in the Bible the conception is of a seed corrupting itself into what it never was. Watch the history of any spiritual work, you will find it begins magnificently and then fizzles out, and if you are not in the secret, you will say, "What a discouraging business!" The devil would conserve it into a little crystallized compartment and make us worship it, but God sends His forces and disintegrates it into the same kind of failure that the life of His Son was, and then He brings out in fruit something no man ever dreamt of. Christianity is always a forlorn hope in the eyes of the world; it is always dying and bringing forth what it never was.

The Fortune of Misfortune

Philippians 1: 12

The fortune of misfortune! that is Paul's way of looking at his captivity. He does not want them to be depressed on his account, or to imagine that God's purposes have been hindered; he says they have not been hindered, but furthered. The very things which looked so disastrous have turned out to be the most opportune, so that on this account the Apostle's heart is bounding with joy, and the same note of rejoicing is found throughout the whole Letter.

November 18th

Instruments or Servants

Philippians 1: 15

An instrument of God and a servant of God ought to be identical, but our Lord's words in Matthew 7 and Paul's words here are instances where they are not. It does not impair the inspiration of the Gospel to have it preached by a bad man, but the influence of the preacher, worthy or unworthy, apart altogether from his preaching, has a tremendous effect. If I know a man to be a bad man the sinister influence of his personality neutralizes altogether the effect of God's message through him to me; but let me be sure that my intuition springs from my own relationship to God and not from human suspicion.

November 19th

Holiness Imparted

Philippians 3: 9

The only holiness there is, is the holiness derived through faith, and faith is the instrument the Holy Spirit uses to organize us into Christ. But do not let us be vague here. Holiness, like sin, is not a series of acts, it is a disposition. A man can act holily, but he has not a holy *disposition*. A saint has had imparted to him the disposition of holiness, therefore holiness is to be the characteristic of the life here and now. Entire sanctification is the end of the disposition of sin, but only the beginning of the life of the saint, then comes growth in holiness. The process of sanctification begins at the moment of birth from above, and is consummated on the unconditional surrender of my right to myself to Jesus Christ. The time that elapses between new birth and entire sanctification depends entirely on the individual.

God Can Undo the Past

Joel 2: 25

In a crisis leave everything to God, shut out every voice saving the voice of God and the psalm of your own deliverance; make it your duty to remain true to both these voices.

In the life of a saint tribulation does this supernatural thing —it brings back innocence with experience; in the natural world experience brings cunning and craftiness. We sit down under the tyranny of a devil's lie and say, "I can't undo the past:" you cannot, but God can. God can make the past, as far as our spiritual life is concerned, as if it had never been and even in its worst features He can make it bring out the 'treasures of darkness.'

"Jacob Was Left Alone"

Genesis 32: 24

"And Jacob was left alone" (v. 24).

This phrase is significant because in his loneliness Jacob goes through the decisive struggle of his life. We are dealing in this chapter with Jacob the giant, not with the mean man. ". . . and there wrestled a man with him until the breaking of the day." Jacob tried to strangle the answer to his own prayer; his wrestling represents the human fighting with God. The noblest ones in God's sight are those who do not struggle but go through without demur. Abraham did not wrestle, neither did Isaac; Jacob struggles for everything. If a man has difficulty in getting through to God we are apt to imagine it is an indication of a fine character whereas the opposite is true, he is refusing to yield and is kicking, and the only thing God can do is to cripple him. The characteristics exhibited by Jacob are those of Peter before Pentecost and Saul of Tarsus before his conversion, a mixture of the dastardly and the heroic, the mean and the noble, all jumbled up.

"Jacob Halted on His Thigh"

Genesis 32: 31

Jacob's wrestling means that he did not want to go through the way he knew he must, he had to come to the end of the best of his natural self, to go to the 'white funeral' of his own wisdom, and he struggled in order not to. Then he came to the place where his wisdom was crippled for ever. "And he halted upon his thigh." The symbol is expressive of what it looks like in the eyes of shrewd worldly wisdom to cast yourself unperplexed on God. When we cling to God we learn to kneel for the first time.

If you have never been to 'Peniel' you are sure to come across things that will put your human wisdom into a panic; if you have seen God face to face your circumstances will never arouse any panic in you. We run off at a tangent—anywhere but Peniel where we would see God face to face.

Spirit, Soul, and Body

1 Thessalonians 5: 23

Soul is the rational expression of my personal spirit in my body, the way I reason and think and work. Habits are formed in the soul, not in the spirit, and they are formed in the soul by means of the body. Jesus Christ told His disciples that they must lose their soul, i.e., their way of reasoning and looking at things, and begin to estimate from an entirely different standpoint. For a while a born-again soul is inarticulate, it has no expression; the equilibrium has been upset by the incoming of a totally new spirit into the human spirit, and the reasoning faculties are disturbed. "In your patience possess ye your souls," says Jesus; i.e., the new way of looking at things must be acquired with patience. On the basis of His Redemption Jesus Christ claims that He can put into my personal spirit His own heredity, viz., Holy Spirit; then I have to form character on the basis of that new disposition. God will do everything I cannot do, but He will do nothing He has constructed me to do.

The Cleansing of the Unconscious

Psalm 19; 1 John 1: 7

Cleansing from all sin does not mean conscious deliverance from sin only, it means infinitely more than we are conscious of. The part we are conscious of is walking in the light: cleansing from all sin means something infinitely profounder, it means cleansing from all sin in the sight of God. God never bases any of His work on our consciousness. "Do you mean to tell me that God can search me to the inmost recesses of my dreams, my inmost motives, and find nothing to blame? That God Almighty can bring the winnowing fan of His Spirit and search out my thoughts and imaginations, and find nothing to blame?" Who can stand before God and say, My hands are clean, my heart is pure? Who can climb that hill of the Lord? No man under heaven, saving the man who has been re-adjusted at the Cross of Christ.

The Transforming Power of Regeneration

1 Thessalonians 1: 5

If our body has been the slave of wrong habits physically, mentally and morally, we must get hold of a power big enough to re-make our habits, and that power lies in the word 'Regeneration.' "If any man be in Christ, he is a new creature," that means this marvellous thing—that I may be loosened from every wrong habit I have formed if only I will obey the Spirit of God. Immediately I do obey, I find I can begin to form new habits in accordance with His commands, and prove physically, mentally and morally that I am a new creation. That is why it is so necessary to receive the Holy Spirit, then when God gives a command it is sufficient to know He has told me to do it and I find I can do it. Frequently God has to say to us—"Say no more to Me on this matter; don't everlastingly cry to Me about this thing, do it yourself, keep your forces together and go forward." God is for you, the Spirit of God is in you, and every place that the sole of your foot shall tread upon, shall be yours.

The Secret of Radiance

Ephesians 5: 14

The joy that Jesus gives is the result of our disposition being at one with His own disposition. The Spirit of God will fill us to overflowing if we will be careful to keep in the light. We have no business to be weak in God's strength.

"Look therefore carefully how ye walk." We have to walk in the light "as He is in the light," keep continually coming to the light, don't keep anything covered up. If we are filled with the life of Jesus we must walk circumspectly, keep the interest in life going, have nothing folded up. The evidence that we are being filled with the life of God is that we are not deceived about the things that spring from ourselves and the things that spring from Jesus Christ. "If you have sinned," says John, "confess it, keep in the light all through."

God Gives the Body: We Form the Habits

Hebrews 10: 5; Colossians 3: 17

The difference between a sentimental Christian and a sanctified saint is just here. The sanctified saint is one who has disciplined the body into perfect obedience to the dictates of the Spirit of God, consequently his body does with the greatest of ease whatever God wants him to do. The sentimental type of Christian is the sighing, tear-flowing, beginning-over-again Christian who always has to go to prayer meetings, always has to be stirred up, or to be soothed and put in bandages, because he has never formed the habit of obedience to the Spirit of God. Our spiritual life does not grow *in spite of* the body, but *because* of the body.

November 28th

Christ, the Context of Scripture

John 5: 39, 40

These verses reveal how a knowledge of the Scriptures may distort the mind away from Jesus Christ. Unless we know the Living Word personally first, the literal words may lead us astray. The only way we can understand the Bible is by personal contact with the Living Word, then the Holy Spirit expounds the literal words to us along the line of personal experience. "The words I speak unto you, they are spirit and they are life." The Jews knew the Scriptures thoroughly, yet their minds were so distorted that when they saw Jesus Christ they said, "He hath a devil." There is a context to the Bible, and Jesus Christ is that Context. The right order is personal relationship to Him first, then the interpretation of the Scriptures according to His Spirit.

November 29th

The Peril of Unfulfilled Vows

Ecclesiastes 5: 2

To make a promise may simply be a way of shirking responsibility. Never pile up promises before men, and certainly not before God. It is better to run the risk of being considered indecisive, better to be uncertain and not promise, than to promise and not fulfil. "Better is it that thou shouldest not vow, than that thou shouldest vow and not pay."

The vices of vowing outweigh the virtues, because vowing is built on a misconception of human nature as it really is. If a man had the power to will pure will, it would be different, but he has not. There are certain things a man cannot do, not because he is bad, but because he is not constituted to do them. We make vows which are impossible of fulfilment because no man can remain master of himself always; there comes a time when the human will must yield allegiance to a force greater than itself, it must yield either to God or to the devil.

The Ultimate Witness—"Unto Me"

Acts 1: 8

When we are born again of the Spirit the note of our testimony is what God has done for us, and rightly so; but the baptism of the Holy Ghost obliterates that for ever. God will never answer our prayer to be baptized by the Holy Ghost for any other reason than to be a witness for Jesus. "Ye shall receive power, after that the Holy Ghost is come upon you: and ye shall be witnesses unto Me . . . ." Not witnesses of what Jesus can do, that is an elementary witness, but 'witnesses unto Me'—you will be instead of Me, you will take everything that happens, praise or blame, persecution or commendation, as happening to Me. No one can stand that unless he is constrained by the majesty of the personal power of Jesus. Paul says I am constrained by the love of Christ, held as in a fever, gripped as by a disease, that is why I act as I do; you may call me mad or sober, I do not care; I am after only one thing—to persuade men of the judgment seat of Christ and of the love of God.

Walking in God's Light

1 John 1: 7

A born-again soul is condemned to holiness; he is not at liberty to do what he likes but only what God likes, a 'bondslave of Jesus'; my relationship to God first, second, and third and all the time. The modern note is that we have sinned against this one and that one: every sin we commit against another is a sin against God, and the Bible brings us face to face with God. Can my salvation stand the glaring light of God? Can my relationship with my fellow men stand the light of God? It has got to one day. That is the way the Spirit of God rouses us up to see that there is no refuge in anything or anyone other than Himself. The whole life must be established in God. The one thing that keeps us right is walking in the light of the great High God.

Search Me, O God

Psalm 139: 23

We make mistakes through not knowing the way we are designed. For instance, people talk about inattention as if it came from the devil, whereas it really arises from a complete misunderstanding of the way we are made. Psalm 139 is a Psalm of introspective intercession, the Psalmist realizes that he is a great deal more that he can grasp, there are deeper depths in him and higher heights than in the sea or the mountains; but he does not leave himself in abstractions, he comes straight back to God, "Search me, O God, and know my heart."

Disposition and Character

Philippians 2: 12

A man must make his own character, but he cannot make his disposition. Naturally our disposition is gifted to us by heredity, and in Regeneration God gives to us the disposition of His Son. Neither when we are born into this world nor when we are born again are we given character: character is the thing we must make, and it works in the same way when we are spiritual as when we are natural. You cannot estimate a man's character by isolated things, but only by the main trend of the life. Character represents the difference between disposition and the working of it out actually.

From the Old to the New

2 Corinthians 5: 17

The Bible reveals that the natural virtues are remnants of what the human race was as God designed it, i.e., the natural virtues belong to an order that is no longer appearing. The 'man of old' has to pass and the 'new man' has to dominate, but in the meantime there is chaos. The great thing to realize is that our physical nature is the same after we are born again as we were before, the difference is in the ruling disposition.

God and My Character

Psalm 18: 25, 26

The revelation of God to me is determined by the state of my character toward God. "With the merciful Thou wilt shew Thyself merciful;" says the Psalmist, "and with the perverse Thou wilt shew Thyself forward" (Psalm 18: 25–6). If we persist in being stiff-necked toward God, we will find He is stiff-necked toward us; if we show ourselves meek toward God, He will reveal Himself as gentle toward us.

The Danger of Disloyalty

Psalm 73: 25-28

None of us is free from disloyalty unless we are absolutely loyal. We are always on the wrong line when we come to God with a pre-occupied mind, because a preoccupied mind springs from a disloyal heart: "I don't want to do God's will, what I want is for God to give me permission to do what I want to do." That is disloyalty, and the experience of Psalm 106: 15 is the inevitable result—"And He gave them their request; but sent leanness into their soul."

At the Foot of Jacob's Ladder

John 1: 51

Jacob is the man who represents life as it is. The world is not made up of saints or of devils, but of people like you and like me, and our real home is at the foot of Jacob's ladder with the sneak. Never say that God intended a man to have a domain of dreaming, mighty visions of God, and at the same time be dead towards God in his actual life. Jesus Christ claims that He can make the real and the actual one, as they were in His own life.

The Road Back to Yesterday
Joel 2: 25

Through the Redemption God undertakes to deal with a man's past, and He does it in two ways: by forgiving him, and by making the past a wonderful culture for the future. The forgiveness of God is a bigger miracle than we are apt to think. It is impossible for a human being to forgive; and it is because this is not realized that we fail to understand that the forgiveness of God is a miracle of Divine grace. Do I really believe that God cannot, dare not, must not forgive me my sin without its being atoned for? If God were to forgive me my sin without its being atoned for, I should have a greater sense of justice than God. It is not that God says in effect, "I will pay no more attention to what you have done." When God forgives a man, He not only alters him but transmutes what he has already done.

The Divine Paradox, Solved in the Incarnation
Revelation 5: 6

"*I beheld a Lamb!*" In the Book of Isaiah a paradox of a similar nature occurs; the prophet has been looking for some great conquering army of the Lord and instead he sees a lonely Figure, "travelling in the greatness of his strength," and he asks "Who is this that cometh from Edom?" If you take all the manifestations of God given in the Old Testament you find them a mass of contradiction —now God is pictured as a Man, now as a Woman, now as a lonely Hero, now as a suffering Servant, and until we come to the New Testament these conflicting characteristics but add confusion to our conception of God. But immediately we see Jesus Christ, we find all the apparent contradictions blended in one unique Personality.

Tempted in All Points

Hebrews 4: 15

Jesus Christ took on Him our physical frailty, not our moral frailty—that would mean He had moral perversity on the inside; and in this physical frame He lived a spotlessly holy life. If Jesus Christ had not partaken of our human frailty He could never have been tempted, it would have been a pretence; but He is not tempted 'in all points like as we are' before we have been made 'His brethren' by sanctification (*see* ch. 2: 11). Every temptation possible to us after that experience, He knows all about, and we can be more than conquerors through Him.

The Way Prepared, the Glory Revealed

Isaiah 40: 3-5

Unless we prepare on the outside in accordance with the inner vision we are not in God's order. John the Baptist prepared the way of the Lord historically, but take it personally—how many valleys have I exalted, and how many mountains have I made low? How many mountains of prejudice have I put out of the way? If we prepare on the outside we enable God to plant His glory there, and the first thing we have to do is to go dead against our ingrained prejudices which put a barrier round about us. If I will *do* in accordance with what God has made me *be*, He will reveal His glory.

December 12th
The Blessing of the Pure in Heart
Matthew 5: 8

The vision of God's purpose comes from a pure heart, from acute intellect; the condition is—the inner life right with God. An illiterate old woman with a pure heart has a greater insight into the purposes of God than a prime minister. If the prime minister has a pure heart as well as powerful intellect, then you have a man like Isaiah, a giant for God. The sanctification-metaphysic underlies everything. The opportunity is given to us all to be the choice souls. The God who guides the stars, unhasting and unresting, will as assuredly fulfil what He has promised.

December 13th
God's Message to a Disobedient People
Isaiah 40: 1, 2

"Comfort ye, comfort ye My people, saith your God." Notice the 'My,' and remember that they were a disobedient people, and yet God is 'not ashamed to be called their God.' It is not the love of God for a pure saint, but the love of God for a sin-stained people. He might well have been ashamed of them on account of their sin and degradation, but His voice comes in all its amazing wonder— "Speak ye comfortably" ("to the heart of," R.V. marg.) "to Jerusalem, . . ." It is a wonderful picture of what God does in the Atonement.

Help From on High

Psalm 18: 16; Ephesians 2: 6

The Lord Jesus Christ is the Highest; is there anyone higher to you? Your life is never safeguarded until Jesus is seen to be the Highest. Past experience will not keep you, neither will deliverance from sin; the only safeguarding power is the Highest. If there is a breath of confidence anywhere else there will be disaster, and it is by the mercy of God that you are allowed to stumble or be pain-smitten, until you learn that He does it all—*He* keeps you from stumbling. *He* raises you up and keeps you. *He* sends from above and delivers you.

Gracious Manifestation of the Life of God

Genesis 26: 12–22

The only right a Christian has is the right to give up his rights. This is the tender grace which is usually looked upon as an exhibition of lack of gumption. The embarrassing thing about Christian graces is that immediately you imitate them they become nauseating, because conscious imitation implies an affected preference for certain qualities, and we produce frauds by a spurious piety. To have the attitudes of life without the life itself is a fraud; to have the life itself imitating the best Pattern of that life is normal and right (*see* 1 Peter 2: 21–3). All the qualities of a godly life are characteristic of the life of God; you cannot imitate the life of God unless you have it, and then the imitation is not conscious, but the unconscious manifestation of the real thing.

Concentration on the Highest

Isaiah 50: 10

Whenever there is a complication in your circumstances do nothing until you see the Highest, not sometimes, but always (cf. Isaiah 50: 10). Can you see the Lord in your thinking? If not, suspend your judgment until you can. Can you see the face of Jesus in your affections? If not, restrain them until you can. Can you see God in your circumstances? If not, do nothing until you can. Our Lord can trust anything to the man or woman who has seen Him.

"*Set* your affection on things above," says Paul, gather in the stray impulses and fix them. The spiritual life is not impulsive; we are impulsive when we are not spiritual. In every experience the standard is our Lord Himself, and He was never impulsive; impulse was the one thing He always checked. Impulse has to be trained and turned into intuition by discipline.

December 17th

"Whatsoever Things Are Lovely"

Philippians 4: 8

The word 'lovely' has the meaning of juicy and delicious. We have the idea that our duty must always be disagreeable, and we make any number of duties out of diseased sensibilities. If our duty is disagreeable, it is a sign that we are in a disjointed relationship to God. If God gave some people a fully sweet cup, they would go carefully into a churchyard and turn the cup upside down and empty it, and say, "No, that could never be meant for me." Duty is the daughter of God. Never take your estimate of duty after a sleepless night, or after a dose of indigestion; take your sense of duty from the Spirit of God and the word of Jesus. There are people whose lives are diseased and twisted by a sense of duty which God never inspired; but once let them begin to think about the things of loveliness, and the healing forces that will come into their lives will be amazing. The very essence of godliness is in the things of loveliness; think about them, says Paul.

'Things of Good Report'

Philippians 4: 8

When we do think about the things of good report we shall be astonished to realize where they are to be found; they are found where we only expected to find the opposite. When our eyes are fixed on Jesus Christ we begin to see qualities blossoming in the lives of others that we never saw there before. We see people whom we have tabooed and put on the other side exhibiting qualities we have never exhibited, although we call ourselves saved and sanctified. Never look for other people to be holy; it is a cruel thing to do, it distorts your view of yourself and of others. Could anyone have had a sterner view of sin than Jesus had, and yet had anyone a more loving tender patience with the worst of men than He had? The difference in the attitude is that Jesus Christ never expected men to be holy; He knew they could not be: *He came to make men holy.* All He asks of men is that they acknowledge they are not right, then He will do all the rest.

Joy Among the Unexpected

Psalm 126: 1–6

The characteristic of this passage is the unexpectedness of the happenings. "Then was our mouth filled with laughter, and our tongue with singing." We never dreamed that such a thing would happen to us! This attitude of mind frequently comes by the way of a calamity. Many a man has had his soul restored in the valley of the shadow, not in the green pastures. There are clouds we fear to enter, but on the inside of these clouds is the suddenness of real light. We get the evidence of this on the threshold of real sorrow and difficulty, there is the suddenness of real light and a discernment of things that was unsought, which we could get in no other way.

December 20th

A Second Adam, to the Rescue Came

Luke 1: 35

"The Holy Ghost shall come upon thee, and the power of the Highest shall overshadow thee: therefore also that holy thing which shall be born of thee shall be called the Son of God."

The New Testament reveals that the birth of Jesus was an advent, not a beginning—an advent that put Him on the plane, humanly speaking, that Adam was on. The first Adam and the last Adam came direct from the hand of God.

God did not create Adam holy, He created him innocent, without self-consciousness (as we understand the word) before God; the one thing Adam was conscious of was God and only of himself in relation to the Being Whose commands he was to fill; the main trend of his spirit was towards God. Adam was intended by God to take part in his own development by a series of moral choices whereby he would transform innocence into holiness. Adam failed to do this. Jesus Christ came on the same platform as Adam and did not fail.

December 21st

Son of God, Son of Man: The God Man

John 1: 1, 14, 18

There are phases of the Life of Our Lord presented in the New Testament that no other Life, so-called, deals with. If you start with the theory that Jesus Christ was a man who became God, you have to leave out any number of New Testament facts; if you say that Jesus Christ was God and His manhood a seeming phase, you have to miss out other facts. The Person of Jesus Christ revealed in the New Testament is unique—God-Man. In Him we deal with God as Man, the God-Man, the Representative of the whole human race in one Person. Jesus Christ is not a Being with two personalities; He is *Son of God*—the exact expression of Almighty God and *Son of Man*—the presentation of God's normal Man.

184

The Purpose of the Incarnation

Matthew 1: 21

Jesus Christ became Incarnate for one purpose, to make a way back to God that man might stand before Him as he was created to do, the friend and lover of God Himself. The Atonement means infinitely more than we can conceive, it means that we can be morally identified with Jesus Christ until we understand what the apostle Paul meant when he said, "I live; yet not I, but Christ liveth in me." All the mighty efficacy of the Death of Jesus, of His Resurrection and Ascension to the right hand of the throne of God, is implanted into us by regeneration. And the lowest and most sin-stained can go that way. The measure of the salvation of Jesus is not that it does for the best man we know, but that it does for the worst and most sin-stained. There is no son of man that need despair, Jesus Christ can reproduce His saving work in any and every man, blessed be the Name of God!

The Word Made Weak

John 1: 14

If you look upon Jesus Christ from the common sense standpoint you will never discern who He is; but if you look upon Him as God 'manifested in the flesh' for the purpose of putting the whole human race back to where God designed it to be, you get the meaning of the Redemption. To the common sense standpoint of His own day Jesus Christ was 'the carpenter's son' (*see* Matthew 13: 55). We do not deal with Jesus Christ as the Carpenter of Nazareth: we deal with the Carpenter of Nazareth as *God manifested in the flesh*.

Why the Second Adam Came
Romans 5: 15

When Jesus Christ, the last Adam, came it was not men's external sins He aimed at, but something more fundamental, viz., the heredity of sin—my claim to my right to myself. The Redemption deals with the thing no man can deal with, his heredity. Apart from Jesus Christ I am always more than mastered by sin. ". . . sold under sin," says Paul.

"Him who knew no sin He made to be sin on our behalf;" The revelation is not that Jesus Christ was punished for our sins, but that He was *made to be sin*. The Son of God became the very thing which had severed man from God, and becoming it, He put it away.

'O, Come to My Heart, Lord Jesus'
Galatians 1: 15, 16; 4: 19

Every man is meant to be the 'Bethlehem' of the Son of God by the regenerative power of Redemption. Just as the historic Son of God became Incarnate in the Virgin Mary—"that holy thing which shall be born of thee shall be called the Son of God"—so the Son of God is formed in the life of the individual saint by the supernatural grace of God (Gal. 4: 19). Are we willing to submit to the 'new man' that is formed in us until our natural life is transfigured by His personal indwelling? It has nothing to do with our eternal salvation; it has everything to do with our temporal value to God. All most of us are concerned about is being saved from hell only and being put right for heaven. But there is something infinitely grander than that. We are given the marvellous chance of giving up our right to ourselves to Jesus Christ so that we may become the devoted bondslaves of God Who saves us so supernaturally.

Christ Breaks In

Luke 1: 68

There are those who say there is no such thing as the supernatural incoming of Jesus Christ, either in history or in the human heart. Our Lord Jesus Christ is not Someone Who has sprung from human nature by evolution: He is Someone Who has come crashing into our human nature by the superb miracle of the Incarnation. The supernatural is the only explanation of our lives if we are right with God, and at any moment God may tumble our lives up as He likes. The question is, Are we willing to let Him? We have to maintain our personal relationship to God in Christ Jesus, no matter what happens. The one thing that is of value to God in a human life is a personal relationship of holiness to God, and every part of physical, mental, moral life and of Christian work that is not so related will be desolated and burnt as rubbish.

Dust and Deity

Genesis 1: 27; 2: 7

Genesis 2: 7 reveals that man is made up of dust and Divinity. This means that in practical psychology we must always make allowance for the incalculable. You cannot exhaust man's nature by examining his 'dust' qualities, nor by describing him in terms of poetic sentiment, for after you have described as much as you can, there is always an incalculable element to be taken into account. There is more than we know, therefore we cannot deal with ourselves as machines. One part of ourselves must be dealt with as a machine, and the more we deal with it as a machine the better; but to try and sum up a man as a machine only is to miss out the bigger part. Or to say that man is altogether a spiritual being without anything mechanical in him is to miss out the incalculable element that cannot be summed up. These two things, dust and Divinity, make up man. 'Dust' is man's glory, not his shame; it has been the scene of his shame. but it was designed to be his glory.

The Only True Liberty

John 8: 36; Galatians 5: 1

We have to present the liberty of Christ, and we cannot do it if we are not free ourselves. There is only one liberty, the liberty of Jesus Christ at work in my conscience enabling me to do what is right. If we are free with the liberty wherewith Christ makes us free, slowly and surely those whom we influence will begin to be free with the same freedom. Always keep your own life measured by the standard of Jesus Christ; bow your neck to His yoke alone and to no other yoke whatever; and see that you never bind any yoke on others that Jesus Christ Himself does not place. It takes a long time to get us out of imagining that unless people see as we do they must be wrong. That is never Jesus Christ's view. Our true sympathy lies with the One Who is absolute tenderness, and every now and again God gives us the chance of being the rugged stuff that He might be the tender One. We have to be sacramental elements in the Lord's hands.

Man, After God's Pattern

John 1: 4; 1 John 1: 2

"In Him was life; and the life was the light of men" (John 1: 4). Why did Jesus live thirty-three years if all He came to do was to die for sin? He lived thirty-three years because He had to show what a normal man after God's pattern was like. He died that through His death we might have the source of life that was in Him (Romans 5: 17). That is why it is so absurd to say, "I accept Jesus as a Teacher only." Try to apply the teachings of Jesus to your life without an understanding of His Death and you will find it cannot be done; it would either make you commit suicide or take you to the Cross and give you an understanding of why it was necessary for Him to die.

Our God, a Consuming Fire
Hebrews 12: 29

"Behold, your house is left unto you desolate." Twice before Jesus had said, "My Father's house," the solemn application being that God hands individuals as well as nations over to a desecrated temple which He calls 'your house.' We need to bear in mind that chaos and wrath are the foundation of the life of every man who does not live in communion with God.

". . . everlasting fire, prepared for the devil and his angels." God's holiness never alters its attitude to devilishness; as long as God endures, He endures as 'everlasting fire' to the devil. God is 'a consuming fire' and if we side with the devil we shall know His burning. Divine fire as opposed to natural fire, burns the fiercer the farther you get away from it; when you get nearer to God, His burning becomes a comfort.

The Final Vision of the Exalted Lord
Matthew 28: 16–20

By His Ascension Our Lord raises Himself to glory, He becomes omnipotent, omniscient and omnipresent. All the splendid power, so circumscribed in His earthly life, becomes omnipotence; all the wisdom and insight, so precious but so limited during His life on earth, becomes omniscience; all the unspeakable comfort of the presence of Jesus, so confined to a few in His earthly life, becomes omnipresence, He is with us all the days.

What kind of Lord Jesus have we? Is He the All-powerful God in our present circumstances, in our providential setting? Is He the All-wise God of our thinking and our planning? Is He the Ever-present God, 'closer than breathing, nearer than hands or feet'? If He is, we know what it means to 'abide under the shadow of the Almighty.'

INDEX OF SCRIPTURE REFERENCES

OLD TESTAMENT

NEW TESTAMENT

NEW TESTAMENT